THE
PASSION
OF
INTERPRETATION

LITERARY
CURRENTS
IN
BIBLICAL
INTERPRETATION

EDITORS

Danna Nolan Fewell
Perkins School of Theology,
Southern Methodist University, Dallas TX
David M. Gunn
Columbia Theological Seminary, Decatur GA

EDITORIAL ADVISORY BOARD

THE
PASSION
OF
INTERPRETATION

W.   D O W   E D G E R T O N

•

WESTMINSTER/JOHN KNOX PRESS
Louisville, Kentucky

THE PASSION OF INTERPRETATION

© 1992 W. Dow Edgerton

First edition

Published by Westminster/John Knox Press,
Louisville, Kentucky

This book is printed on acid-free paper that meets the American National Standards Institute Z39.48 standard. ∞

PRINTED IN THE UNITED STATES OF AMERICA
2 4 6 8 9 7 5 3 1

Library of Congress Cataloging-in-Publication Data

Edgerton, W. Dow, 1948-
  The passion of interpretation / W. Dow Edgerton. — 1st ed.
    p.   cm. — (Literary currents in biblical interpretation)
  Includes bibliographical references and indexes.
  ISBN 0-664-25394-6 (alk. paper)

  1. Bible—Criticism, interpretation, etc. 2. Bible as literature. I. Title. II. Series.
BS511.2.E34 1992
220.6'01—dc20   92-30203

To Rose Marie and Dow Edgerton
with deepest gratitude

PERMISSIONS

CONTENTS

SERIES PREFACE

New currents in biblical interpretation are emerging. Questions about origins—authors, intentions, settings—and stages of composition are giving way to questions about the literary qualities of the Bible, the play of its language, the coherence of its final form, and the relations between text and readers.

Such literary criticism is rapidly acquiring sophistication as it learns from major developments in secular critical theory, especially in understanding the instability of language and the key role of readers in the production of meaning. Biblical critics are being called to recognize that a plurality of readings is an inevitable and legitimate consequence of the interpretive process. By the same token, interpreters are being challenged to take responsibility for the theological, social, and ethical implications of their readings.

Biblical interpretation is changing on the practical as well as the theoretical level. More readers, both inside and outside the academic guild, are discovering that the Bible in literary perspective can powerfully engage people's lives. Communities of faith where the Bible is foundational may find that literary criticism can make the Scripture accessible in a way that historical criticism seems unable to do.

Within these changes lie exciting opportunities for all who seek contemporary meaning in the ancient texts. The goal of the series is to encourage such change and such search, to breach the confines of traditional biblical criticism, and to open channels for new currents of interpretation.

—THE EDITORS

1

STORIES
OF
INTERPRETATION

INTERPRETATION IN CRISIS

nterpretation is in crisis. So many questions which once seemed settled, so many foundations which once seemed secure, so many agreements which once seemed firm, have come apart. Issues which go to the bedrock of interpretation have opened deep fissures.

The roots of our crisis are many: philosophical, political, social, theological, economic, military, scientific, critical, sexual, racial, psychological. The possible descriptions of the crisis are many, as well, and the description one prefers will doubtless depend upon the conceptual and experiential roots a person has most deeply struck. There may be no description adequate to what is converging, only descriptions of this force or that; call it a crisis of crises.

Although issues of this sort always seem to have the ring of specialized arguments far from the life of real communities, the crisis does indeed reach deeply into the real life of real communities. What is at stake in a crisis of interpretation is fundamental to human community, for what is at stake are basic issues of identity and meaning. What is the story that tells us the truth? Who are we and how do we know? Upon what reliable meaning can we found our life? What meaning is adequate to the life we know and claim in our own time? What does it mean to have a sacred text? How do we sift between the truth of our texts and the truth of our lives? Such questions are as basic as bread.

This is to say that the crisis is full of help as well as danger. We tend to become aware of our intellectual and spiritual foundations only when they are shaken. When they are shaken one recognizes that they have been *built*, and like anything that is built, could be destroyed, and could be built differently. The danger comes in the real possibility of disintegration. Communities do lose themselves, become chaotic, suffer and inflict suffering. The help comes in the new building that happens, especially when many hands—often hands which never were allowed to help before—turn to the work of discovering new foundations for human life and community.

The contemporary interpretive upheaval has helped to make more visible that interpretation itself *is* a crisis. It begins in crisis, proceeds through crisis, and finally arrives in crisis. It begins in the recognition of a gap between our texts and our lives, a gap which threatens to widen and widen until there is only open sea left between texts and lives going their own ways. It proceeds through holding that gap open, exploring the particularity, the difference, the otherness of the text and its own world. It turns toward the interpreter with questions and possibilities, the need for decision—about the interpreter, about the text, about their relationship.

The language of crisis, choice, will, however, is only a part of the dynamic. For it is not only a work of distinguishing, dividing, and choosing; it is also a work of bringing together, linking, narrating, imagining. If interpretation is a work in which one is *confronted* by an Other, it is as much a work of being *joined* by an Other in a world made together.

INTERPRETATION AND NARRATIVE

In the last twenty years literary criticism in general, and narrative studies in particular, have become increasingly important for many different fields. There has been an explosion of related interdisciplinary work in philosophy, linguistics, history of religions, personality sciences, sociology, human development, and anthropology—not to mention theology. In the broad field of theological studies itself it is difficult to find an area upon which this work has not had a major impact: ethics, pastoral care, systematics, biblical studies, congregational studies, homiletics, history. All of these have been powerfully shaped by new understandings of the nature and function of narrative.

Much of the contemporary reflection on narrative has emerged in response to a dramatic revaluation of narrative's place in human experience.[1] Instead of being seen as a secondary linking of experience and idea, an "after the fact" or "after the idea" operation to put things together, narrative is being recognized as fundamental to human perception and thought. Narrative does not interpret discrete and unrelated experiences into a whole, but is *prior* to perception. Narrative is, in a way, the very medium of perception. As Stephen Crites (1971) has put it, "There is no point so deep in the life of a culture that it is free from the narrative form, nothing prior to narrative upon which narratives depend." Wesley Kort (1989:12) writes, "narrative, rather than a product of originally separated, non-narrative ingredients, is itself originating of those aspects of our world that we abstract from a narrative base and isolate from one another as facts and ideas." Even the critical, scientific, and philosophical ways of reflection, it is maintained, rest upon a foundation of narrative. They begin in narrative, depend upon narrative, and always bear the trace of narrative within them.

We could argue, then, that every method of interpretation has a story at its root, acknowledged or not, or a story at its flower, told or not yet told. Talk about interpretive method is finally a way of telling a story, or reflecting upon a story; it is the work of interpretation. As in the usual sense of story, there are characters with their various desires or needs, shaped in their particular strength and weakness. There is a world of possibilities and impossibilities. There is a search with a goal. There are antagonists—perhaps other interpreters, perhaps the text itself, perhaps the sheer hazard of the interpretive landscape. There are advances and retreats in the adventure—a crisis, a climax, a denouement, some conclusion. It may all be tragic or comic or romantic or ironic, resolved or unresolved; whatever a usual sort of story can be, a story of interpretation can be, as well.[2]

Story and interpretation, nevertheless, are two different kinds of discourse. There will always remain between them a "formal incommensurability," which prevents either from being reduced to the other. As responses to human experience, story and interpretation (or theory) have different goals and justify themselves by different standards. If the goal of a theory is to offer the general principles, the goal of story is to offer the concrete, the particular (Crites 1975:26). Although story may be full of (or even about) ideas, it belongs not to the sphere of ideas, but to the sphere of characters, places, things, events, images. It is because of this difference that story both provokes and frustrates interpretation. It is also because of this that story may renew interpretation, which may return to the same story again and again to discover new meaning.

In one sense, a story of interpretation veils the principles, the method, and the assumptions at work. Rather than being given and applied, they must be deduced, proposed, argued into the open. Only then do the implications spread beyond the particular account. Only then does the interpreter return to the story of interpretation to read it in the light of these implications.

In another sense, a story of interpretation is an unveiling. Now we can see what interpretation actually does; now we can see where it leads; now is made plain what was only a possibility, a speculation. The story's concreteness sends the interpreter back to the principles to read them by new light. Both senses are true. In the tension between them, in the rhythm and play of the veiling and unveiling, stories of interpretation are their most intriguing and troubling. To amend Paul Ricoeur (1967: 347) slightly, "the story gives rise to thought."

There is a kind of reflection which begins with problems, questions, and ideas (the general), and then moves toward consideration of events, objects, texts, stories (the particular). There is a kind of reflection which moves in the other direction. It begins with stories and images, and asks how they engage what one thinks and knows and does. What is it like to think within the boundaries and possibilities of this "world" or these signs? The work here is of this second kind.

14

We are concerned here with stories of interpretation and what understanding of interpretation might emerge through our encounters. We are first of all concerned with exegesis or "explanation" of specific stories, to use the word in Ricoeur's (1978:137-9) sense—that is, exegesis undertaken as an uncovering of the "immanent design" present in each story, the dominant narrative elements, the language, the composition. To propose such a design is to propose the "world" of the story, and the ways of being that are disclosed by it. "Texts speak of possible worlds and of possible ways of orienting oneself in those worlds . . . And interpretation becomes the grasping of the world-propositions opened up" (Ricoeur 1978:144). We are secondly concerned with an interpretation of the interplay of these elements as it pertains to the work of interpretation itself. That is to say, we are concerned with hermeneutics and how the particularity of the story and its world leads to consideration of what interpretation is and does.

A "world" is a representation of a reality. It is a small universe in which action, narration, and meaning is possible. In this world there are characters who act out their needs or desires within the given possibilities and limits. They display their particular vices and virtues. They combine and conflict, and enact their story through a peculiar law and logic, and we see what happens when it all comes together. It is a *narrated* world, which means that there is also always a teller of the story. Hidden or revealed, honest or dishonest, within or above, seeing everything or seeing only part—there is a narrator who is as much an aspect of this world as any character. The story-teller decides when and what we shall see and hear, and from what vantage point. Thus, to understand the world one must also ask why it is presented in *this* way. Why are we placed *here* and not *there*? Why do we hear *this* but not *that*? Who does the story-teller take us or make us to be? These are aspects of tone which, in combination with plot, character, and atmosphere, lay the foundations of a narrated world.[3]

To these elements one may add others. What kind of narrative is it? How is it presented to us? It makes a difference, after all, if we suppose a story is history, myth, folk-tale, fiction,

15

scripture, parable, or something else. There are different rules by which each genre plays the game, and it matters which game one supposes is being played. One also may ask about the effect of the specific language—style, vocabulary, sound, rhythm—all the various combinations on the surface of the language. They, too, impress themselves onto the world and shape what it seems to be; they constantly communicate in, under, around, and through, the other elements.

Through such questions as these, we shall explore the worlds our stories put before us, seeking first of all to understand what interpretation is within those worlds, and last of all, what they say to the stories we tell about our own interpretation. Certain assumptions about the nature of interpretation are already evident in these few pages. The figures of Hans-Georg Gadamer and Paul Ricoeur cast long shadows, and I am happy to rest in their shade. But there are others, many others from many places, whose voices can and will be heard in these pages.

The stories for this study are of several different types. We will read a rabbinic story, a story from the Hebrew Bible, a Greek myth, two modern short stories, and a story from the New Testament. They have been chosen because each is concerned with interpretation in a different way. Each one displays the possibilities and dangers of interpretation under its own terms, within its own world, and through its own emblems. Through each story the work of interpretation may be considered as its stands under a special sign, as a particular kind of exegesis.

Why these stories instead of others? In part the choice is based upon subjective judgments of their intrinsic merit. They are fascinating stories to think about; they are complex, powerful, and troubling in their own right. More important, however, is that these stories open onto questions which are among the most difficult of our time. Who may interpret? Who can? What should be read and by whom? Who sets the "canon"? What are the motives of interpretation? What is authority? What does it mean to have a "scripture"? Is there any real difference between the stories we create and stories we take to be true? Is there even anything to *be* interpreted? Is there meaning to texts, or only texts themselves which endlessly replay in different combinations what is already written? Each such question aims at a different aspect of the foundations of interpretation, and each such question has myriad particular nuanced variations. Each *story* presented here leads us toward such questions in a vivid way, and offers us something the questions themselves cannot: a circumscribed "world" within which to imagine and think.

I think and write self-consciously from within western Judeo-Christian tradition. My chief concern is with the interpretation of powerful texts of this tradition, and with the people for whom these texts make a difference. I think and write self-consciously from within the Christian church, in particular, as a pastor and teacher. I am concerned with the person for whom interpretation is both daily bread and holy bread, as ordinary and as miraculous as manna in the wilderness, or the loaves marked by hot stones which the angel left for dismayed Elijah as he slept beneath the broom tree. I am concerned with the community which lives by such interpretation, a community which is now in crisis, and which perhaps must be perpetually in crisis because of its own nature, its own founding stories.

These studies are offered in the hope that they will provide an opportunity to explore dimensions of the passion of interpretation as it confronts us now, in a time when so much is needed, and so much is possible.

2

THE
EXEGESIS
OF
DESIRE

"THIS LIE COMES FROM OLDEN TIMES"

Cattle-rustling robber, carrier of dreams,
Watcher by night who haunts the gates,
Lucky finder, inventor of instruments, singer of myths;
Eraser of traces, reverser of signs,
Counsellor of blindness, deafness, dumbness;
Inventor of fire-sticks, priest of sacrifice,
Night-time prowler who goes through keyholes as a mist;
Coy pretender to weakness,
Bitter, ruthless searcher for place and honor,
Liar, maker of false oaths,
Deceiver with words as well as signs,
Who boldly demands justice for what he knows is untrue;
Manipulator through music,
Giver of gifts which may be stolen back,
Who desires to know,
But has not been given to know
The mind of Zeus on his own,
Lord of wild and tame beasts,
Messenger to the dead:
This is Hermes, the herald of the gods.[1]

t is a deep irony that of all the Greek gods, Hermes should be
herald. It is a deep irony that the one who communicates the
divine will to humankind steals, lies, destroys or distorts signs,

and makes oaths in order to break them. It is also a deep irony that interpretation should be forever linked to his name through the strange word "hermeneutics." Can it really be that interpreting the truths about ourselves also means, somehow, to lie?

Maybe there was simply a mistake somewhere. Somewhere lost in antiquity maybe there was some other god, very different from this one, whose titles were stolen or usurped—or even just mislaid—only to be mistakenly given to the fascinating and bizarre Hermes. Perhaps that is true. Hermes is a thief, after all, who came to his high office through theft. But perhaps there is more than simple contradiction, an arbitrary conjunction of opposites; perhaps it is an *abiding* irony, an abiding and necessary contradiction which will not go away; perhaps there is something about interpretation itself which requires that its embodiment among the gods be as thief, trickster, and liar.

There are so many stories of so many different kinds at work among us and within us. There are those we know and ponder by choice or necessity. There are those of our canon, to which there is a kind of responsibility—a kind of accountability—and by which we interpret other stories. There are also the stories we have forgotten or never quite fixed, stories from which we live without calling them to mind and reflecting upon them. Personal, cultural, religious, and more, they stand in the background of awareness, perhaps an even more powerful canon than the acknowledged one, shaping the ways we sift and sort, determining the viewpoint, the line of sight, and the rhythm by which the eye scans the horizon.

There are yet other stories at work, and at work yet more invisibly and inaudibly. These are the stories we have never heard and never told, never known even in order to forget. Such stories—often quite ancient, whether an antiquity measured in years or depth—nevertheless may lie deeply buried in the labyrinths of language and thought, deeply buried in the field of imagination one takes to be the world. Such stories—invisible, inaudible, elemental, perhaps even untraceable—wield the most subtle power of all because they number among the very threads from which one's tapestry of reality is woven. These are stories, nevertheless, which may be awakened in us, as if we had known them all along, or as if we had been known by them all along. There we may find images, not of who we wish to be, or how we ought to be, but of how we are. Our first study is of this kind of story. We begin with a myth about Hermes, and how he came to be the herald of the gods.

To tell a story about origins is to make a deep claim upon the present. It is done in many different ways and for many different reasons, as has been recognized since ancient times.[2] As part of that broad body called "myth" such stories have been used for quite diverse purposes. They have explained the physical realities of the world, such as air and water. They have personified human qualities and emotions. They have served as the charters of cultures and dynasties. In a more modern gaze, stories of the beginning have been found to supply categories for making sense of the "multitudinousness" of experience, as poetic expressions structuring a cosmos, and as the projection of the human subconscious, or a collective unconscious. Behavior charters, institutional validators, indices of what a people considers important, cultural microcosms, objects and means of worship—some have been found to work in each of these ways, but no myth works in all of them, and none of them can include all myths. A universal theory of myth would seem to be impossible, even if it were desirable (Kirk 1984).

People tell stories about the beginning as a way of telling themselves and others about who they are now, where they are, and why, and what time it is. The stories tell about how far they've fallen, or how far they've come, or how far they have to go. They tell about what *is*, even if the stories themselves are not "believed" by the people who tell them or hear them. "It is not I that lie; this lie comes from olden times," say Malagasy story-tellers as they conclude the recitation of a myth (Doniger O'Flaherty 1988:25). The story need not be true to be real, for a myth "is not so much a true story, but a story upon which truth is based" (Gill 1987; in Doniger O'Flaherty 1988:25).

The French philosopher Émile Chartier wrote in 1911, "If religion is only human, and if its form is man's [sic] form, it follows that everything in religion is true" (1973:7). By "true" he means somehow authentic to human experience, rooted in

20

what human beings have *experienced* to be real at the most immediate, originary level, but then transmuted into image and story. We must stress "somehow" and "transmuted," of course. Whatever the human experience is, as myth it is not given in any direct way, but rather in the form of a story. Presumably, if we could simply say what we mean, we would. If we do not, it is because whatever it is can only be said in *this* way. The story, therefore, becomes a distorted but potentially readable mirror which reflects the only face which cannot be seen directly: the human face that wants to see itself.[3]

If Chartier is correct, then it follows that myths are also dangerous—dangerous to remember and dangerous to forget—and that reading them is dangerous as well. Has humankind never been simply wrong in what it has grasped its experience to be? Have we not inflicted our myths and presumed experience upon one another and thereby worked great suffering and misery? Do we not perpetuate that suffering through repetition of just such storied experience?

Nevertheless, forgetting is more dangerous still. We entrust myth with what cannot be resolved and must not be forgotten. Myths carry an archaeology of the imagination within them, whether social, political, religious, or personal. The beginnings, the "arche" of which they speak, however, may be no more distant than last night's dream, or this morning's work, or what I think I see as the next person approaches me in the street. To forget is to risk losing touch with dimensions of experience—be they good or bad, noble or corrupt, full of pain or pleasure—which are humanly real and at work, and which do not go away simply because they are left unspoken. Quite the opposite.

For interpretation, then, a myth about its origins puts to us questions about just what interpretation is, where it comes from, where it leads. As an interpreter I stand self-consciously within certain traditions *of* interpretation and certain traditions *about* interpretation; that is, there are practices of interpretation which I inherit, and there are beliefs about the work itself. The false prophet, the lying priest, the counterfeit apostle—these are figures my tradition teaches me to despise or ridicule. Haaman, priests of Baal, prophets who tell lies the rulers want to hear, opportunistic preachers who call on the name of a god they do not really know—these remain as warnings of the dangerous risk of presumption interpretation always presents within in the community, and the curse which hangs over the interpreter who causes the community to stumble and fall. "Occasions for stumbling are bound to come, but woe to anyone by whom they come! It would be better for you if a millstone were hung around your neck and you were thrown into the sea than for you to cause one of these little ones to stumble" (Luke 17:1-2).

Hermes, therefore, as a thief, liar, and distorter of signs is an offense to me, and I wish to deny that he and I have anything to do with one another. My tradition, however, has taught me something else: when I am offended, I must look closely and see if what offends me does so because it has uncovered dimensions of myself which I do not care to acknowledge.

"Wherever the truth is," as Augustine wrote, "it is the Lord's." Maybe there is truth about interpretation to be found in the radical oppositions of Hermes, herald of the gods. Maybe if we trace the peculiar constellation of acts, words, and desires this figure puts before us it will lead to something foundational about the work and the experience of interpretation.

THE SCANDALOUS GODLING

Of Hermes sing, O muse, the son of Zeus and Maia . . .
Born at dawn, by midday he played his lyre,
and at evening he stole the cattle of far-shooting Apollon,
on the fourth of the month, the very day mighty Maia bore him.

The best place to meet this god is in a work called the "Hymn to Hermes." The "Hymn" is part of an ancient collection of writings—hymns to the Olympian gods—traditionally attributed to Homer. The actual author and date of the writing has proven impossible to establish; the seventh century BCE is a useful, if undependable, date to conjure with. The "Hymn to Hermes" has very few parallels or variations, and where they exist, dependence upon the "Hymn" has been uncertain at best (see, e.g., Allen and Sikes 1904). There are other sources for various Hermes traditions, but this is the chief literary source, and

22

certainly the most extensive and self-conscious account of the god's deeds and character to have come down to us from those ancient times.[4] The "Hymn" comprises some 580 lines of narrative poetry telling of Hermes' heritage and birth, his strange conflict with Apollo, and his appointment by Zeus to be the herald of the gods.

The messenger of the immortals, the narrator solemnly intones as the poem begins, is the same uncanny infant who was a "shrewd and coaxing schemer, cattle-rustling thief, bringer of dreams," and who now watches by night and haunts the gates. Conceived at night, with the furtive and cheating Zeus as a father, and the nymph Maia for a mother (who lived apart from the gods), Hermes began on the outside, on the margin: the margin of divine society, the margin of day and night, the margin of the fantastic, where "uncanny deeds came to pass" (l.12).

The story proper begins with Hermes' birth to Maia. He was a fantastic child, an incarnation of energy and impatience. There would be no home or cradle for him, except as a place to hide. Scarcely born, Hermes leaped up from his cradle with no explanation to go in search of Apollo's cattle. (Apollo was the mightiest of Zeus's sons.[5]) So Hermes' story begins with searching, and it is a restless story even to the end. The young god's eye seems always turned toward the horizon of the future. Everything is valued for what advantage it may bring, what leverage it gives upon the future. The present is not for arrival, but departure; it is a threshold across which one steps. As the story of his conflict with Apollo grows, whatever devices Hermes employs—inventions, technical skill, deception, lies, performance, oaths—are for the sake of the future. It is from the future that value comes; it is the future which justifies the present.

Hermes was not only the god of tricks and deception; he was also the god of the windfall, the lucky find. His first discovery upon stepping over the threshold of Maia's cave was a tortoise. "An omen of great luck," he declared, as indeed it was; seized and killed, its shell was made into the first lyre, the first of the infant's ingenious inventions, and in the end, a crucial weapon. Of such inventions, such "techne," Hermes was also god. Then craving for meat, the fantastic child ventured out at nightfall in search of cattle, covering himself in darkness the way robbers do.

Hastening from Kyllene in the south to the mountains of Pieria, in the north, where the divine cattle grazed, Hermes cut out fifty cows belonging to Apollo. To cover his trail, he reversed the hooves of the cattle and made for himself wonderful and intricate sandals whose print resembled neither man nor woman, nor animal of any known kind (II. 75-80; cf. II. 219-25).

> Then the son of Maia, sharp-eyed Argeiphontes,
> cut off from the herd fifty head of loud-lowing cattle.
> Through the sand place he drove them on a beguiling route,
> turning their hoofprints round. Mindful of the artful ruse,
> he reversed their hoofs, setting the front part backward
> and the back part frontward and opposite to his own course.
> And forthwith on the sandy beach he plaited sandals
> of wicker-work, wondrous things of unimaginable skill . . .

There was, however, a witness: Hermes had been seen by an old vine-keeper. To protect his theft, his trick, and his identity, the infant god commanded the old man to be blind, deaf, and dumb to what had happened. Then Hermes drove the cattle on under cover of his accomplice, night. At last he reached the Alpheios river, where Hermes grazed the herd and hid them in his barn.

Hermes next invented fire sticks, and single-handedly dragged and slaughtered two cows, a feat which even the "Hymn" depicts as fantastic. He skinned them, roasted them, and set out the meat for a feast. But then came a strange turn. Twelve portions of sacrifice were divided, and although he craved meat—supposedly the purpose of the night-time raid—the infant's "manly soul prevailed." The sacrifice was accomplished all in "proper order," and Hermes left it as a sacrifice, unconsumed. At dawn the thief returned to Maia's cave. He slipped through the keyhole as a mist, and returned to his cradle like an innocent newborn. Maia, however, took notice of what had happened and began to scold him for his shamelessness.

"What is this, you weaver of schemes?
Whence in the dead of night are you coming, clothed in shame-
    lessness?
Go back! Your father planted you to be a vexing care among
    [mortals] and deathless gods."
And Hermes spoke to her with calculated words:
"Mother, why do you fling these words at me as at an
    infant . . . ?
But I shall be master of whatever skill is best
to provide for you and me forever; we shall not suffer,
as you bid me, to stay right here and be
the only two immortals not plied with gifts and prayers . . .
And if my father does not allow me this, I shall surely
    try to be, as I no doubt can, the chief of robbers . . ."
                    (ll. 155-6, 160-3, 166-9, 174-5)

Hermes answered Maia's reproach with the reasons for his
actions: he was determined to provide for them an equal place
among the immortals, with food, and devotion, and honor—by
whatever method it would take. He would practice the greatest
art of all, he said, and he would invade Apollo's sacred pre-
cincts themselves—if it came to that—and carry away even the
sacred vessels.

In the meantime, Apollo had discovered the theft and set
out in search. Encountering the old vine-keeper he heard a
confused report. The old man could not interpret what he had
seen, for it made no sense: a child (or was it a child?), striding
(like a giant?) from side to side of the road, a herd of cows
turned head to tail walking backwards. Neither the old man nor
Apollo could interpret the tracks, signs, or report. Only when he
saw a bird of omen overhead, with whom Apollo had a special
link, did the god know who the thief was.

Apollo then went to Maia's cave to confront Hermes. The
great god and the infant in the cradle argued mightily. Threats,
lies, denials, protests of innocence, oaths, accusations and
counter accusations . . . Hermes was a perfect liar, perfect in
false swearing, perfect in his ridicule of the truth about his
action. Apollo was not deceived, however, and seized the
infant.

Friend, I do think you are a scheming rogue,
and the way you talk you must often have bored your way
into well-built houses and stripped [many] of their possessions,
as you quietly pack away their belongings . . .
But come, lest this be your last and final sleep,
come down from the cradle, you comrade of dark night.
From now on you shall have this honor among the immortals,
to be called the chief of robbers all your days. (ll. 282-5, 289-92)

In self-defense Hermes sent forth "an omen, a hardy effort
of the belly and a reckless messenger" (ll. 295-6), to persuade
Apollo to release him. Hermes, although he was the one who
had lied and sworn falsely, then proposed that the two lay their
case before Zeus and let him judge.

Zeus was the first to recognize the child as one "who looks
like a herald" (l. 331), but remained silent as to the reasons for
his choice of words. Apollo put forward his case, the true case,
but even to Zeus Hermes lied, "I am all for the truth and know
not how to lie" (369), and in many arguments he insisted upon
innocence. Zeus, however, was unconvinced. Laughing at the
child's wiles and skillful denials, he ordered that the cattle be
restored. Defeated for the moment, Hermes led Apollo to them.

As Apollo and the child stood before the herd, however,
Hermes picked up his tortoise-shell lyre and began to play.

His voice came out lovely,
and he sang of the immortal gods and of black earth,
how they came to be, and how each received his lot.
Of the gods with his song he first honored Mnemoysyne,
mother of the Muses, for the son of Maia fell to her lot. (ll. 426-30)

Apollo was enchanted by the song, and was seized by a "stub-
born longing." "Your performance is worth fifty cows. I think
we will settle our accounts at peace" (ll. 437-38). For this skill
and virtuosity Apollo promised to bestow renown upon Hermes
and Maia. But Hermes pressed further. Perhaps in exchange for
the beautiful gift of the lyre, Apollo would give him the power
to divine the will of Zeus, that is, the power to prophesy? The
request was not so much asked, as it was hinted.

The question passed for a while as the cows were returned
to the meadow, and as the gods returned to Olympus. Hermes,

still inventing, devised pipes to play, at which point Apollo turned to him and asked him to swear an oath. Apollo was afraid that Hermes would steal his lyre and the bow, and asked him to swear not to do so. Hermes swore, but only with a nod. Thus assured, Apollo made his great bestowal of honor upon Hermes: friendship, the staff of wealth and prosperity which protects from harm—a herald's staff by which "to accomplish all the laws of noble words and deeds which [Apollo would know] from the voice of Zeus" (ll. 531-32) —lordship over wild beasts, dogs, herds and sheep, and the office of sole messenger to Hades. Apollo refused to grant him knowledge of Zeus's will, however, and offered instead a lesser and weirder kind of divination: the help of "three awesome sisters" who, depending upon which sort of frenzy they were in, sometimes lied and sometimes told the truth.

> Thus Lord Apollon showed his love for the son of Maia
> with every kind of affection . . .
> He is companion to all immortals and mortals.
> Little is the profit he brings, and he beguiles endlessly
> the tribes of [mortals] throughout the night. (ll. 574-8)

Cattle-rustling robber, bringer of dreams, watcher by night who haunts the gates, lucky finder, inventor of instruments, singer of myths; eraser of traces, reverser of signs, counsellor of blindness, deafness, dumbness; inventor of fire-sticks, priest of sacrifice, night-time prowler who goes through keyholes as a mist; coy pretender to weakness, bitter, ruthless searcher for place and honor, liar, maker of false oaths, deceiver with words as well as signs, who boldly demands justice for what he knows is untrue; manipulator through music, giver of gifts which may be stolen back, who desires to know but has not been given to know the mind of Zeus on his own, lord of wild and tame beasts, messenger to the dead. This is the herald of the gods.

AT THE BOUNDARIES

In order to appreciate the depth of contradiction the "Hymn" presents, let us recall something of the role of the herald in ancient Greece.[6] The heart of the office was the reliable repetition of what one had been given to say. The herald was the representative, in some sense even the effective presence, of the royal person who had commissioned him or her (there was a feminine form). The herald was entrusted with messages, public proclamations, declarations of law, embassies, matters related to domestic and foreign relations, treaties, and negotiations in time of war. The office was under the protection of the gods, particularly Hermes, and the person of the herald was to be held inviolable. The badge of office, chiefly the staff, was both a sign of power and a claim for protection and hospitality.

The heraldic office carried cultic significance as well. Heralds would be found leading prayers, sacrifices, and intercessions. Norman O. Brown (1947:24-31) connected the herald to certain kinds of magic as well: word-magic, incantation, deciphering written signs, and the staff as a magical rod. In *The Odyssey*, for example, Hermes' wand is one with which "he charms the eyes of [mortals] or wakens whom he wills" (24.3-4; see also 5.43; *Iliad* 24.343). Brown's work, in fact, places magic in the oldest and deepest layer of the god's archaeology. The magician is transformed into a trickster, and the trickster is transformed into a thief. We meet all three in the "Hymn," and indeed they appear as if nothing were more natural than their connection.

The character of Hermes as a thief or patron of thieves is also found in *The Iliad*, although stealthy action may be as much the point there as theft (see *The Iliad* 5.390; 24.24, 109; 10.266). In the scenes in which the gods debate sending Hermes to steal Hector's body, for example, the epithet for Hermes is "the Wayfinder," a frequent designation in Homer, which suggests that the key ability in theft or secret action is the ability to find a path. Pathfinding is also linked, one may argue, to heraldry at a basic level. All mediation requires the ability to cross boundaries and obstacles and to find a way. In addition to the linkages of herald-magic, trickery, and stealthy action/theft, then, the wayfinding also links with both the stealth and herald/mediator functions.

The crossing of boundaries, whether natural or sacred or human, is an essential aspect of all these characteristic actions; and boundaries, in fact, were most important to the character and function of Hermes in popular Greek religion (Burkert 1985:156-57). Hermes' name, it has been argued, derives from the "herma," a heap of stones used to mark territories and boundaries, which may also have served as a roadside shrine. Hermes was god of boundaries, doors, and roads, and of the doings which transpired there. Thus, he was god of commerce within the city, and trade with strangers and enemies, which depended both upon keeping boundaries and crossing them.[7]

The crossing of boundaries may be, of course, a *violation* of boundaries, personal, political, or sacred. In the "Hymn" Hermes violates sacred boundaries in the theft of cattle, as he does again when he kills the hundred-eyed Argos who had been keeping watch over the captive Io. Hermes uses his flute to enchant the ever watchful jailer, then crushes him with a boulder and sets Io free.[8] While this story itself does not find a place in the "Hymn," Hermes' title of Argeiphontes ("Argos-killer") does (l. 73). He threatens to break sacred boundaries, Apollo's shrines, and even at the conclusion of the "Hymn" Apollo appears unsure of Hermes' promise to steal from him no more. Hermes breaks taboos as well as promises (Burkert 1985:157).

For the sources outside the "Hymn" Hermes chief remaining role, and certainly among the most famous, is as the guide of souls to Hades. Thus in the final book of *The Odyssey*, after the tremendous slaughter Odysseus wreaks upon Penelope's violent and plotting suitors, Hermes leads the souls of the slain down to the underworld. As bats squeak when their "rock-hung chain is broken, so with faint cries the shades trailed after Hermes, pure Deliverer" (24.7-9). Hermes knows the way to Hades, and is the (only?) one who also knows the way back. It is Hermes who brings Kore back from the dead, and it is he who accompanies Eurydice in her too-brief journey with Orpheus.[9] Hermes, one could say, is the one who knows the way into the past and back.

There are other appearances of Hermes in the ancient literature, to be sure, but there can be no mistaking that it is the same god. In Hesiod, Hermes gives "lies and persuasive words and cunning ways" to Pandora.[10] In Ovid, there is a variation of Hermes' encounter with the old man. In Homer there are other episodes in which Hermes takes a part. But they all reveal the same character. It is indeed the Hermes who steals, lies, distorts, and swears falsely; it is indeed the Hermes who is the herald of the gods.

THEATER OF DESIRE:
LIES, THEFT, DECEPTION, MEANING

The myth, as we have said, depicts a radical opposition. The herald of the gods who interprets the divine will to humankind is the same one who steals, lies, destroys or distorts signs, and makes oaths in order to break them, for his own gain and for others.

It is not enough to call the oppositions simply an ambiguity or a confused mixture, to say that sometimes interpretation is wrong or mistaken, or even purposely untruthful. It is not enough to say that interpreters are flawed and sometimes evil. These things are reasonably self-evident, I believe, and they point no farther than a caution to the hearer or reader to beware. The opposition is harder and more intractable, and points to the foundation of interpretation.

Could it be that interpretation *necessarily* stands under the sign of Hermes, in all its contradiction? Could it be that interpretation *must* stand under that sign if it is to tell the truth about itself and what it does? Is there, perhaps a deep dialectic of deception and truth fundamental to interpretation? All interpretation, the "logic" of the myth suggests, is founded upon desire. In the service of this desire interpretation unfolds as a theft, a purposeful distortion of signs, a lie about the act, and the breaking of an oath. Let us retrace the steps of the story with the question of interpretation in mind.

> Craving for meat
> he leaped from the fragrant dwelling and went for scouting,
> pondering some bold wile in his mind, such as [those]
> who are bandits pursue when dark night falls. (ll. 64-7)
> I shall be master of whatever skill is best
> to provide for you and me forever; we shall not suffer,
> as you bid me, to stay right here and be
> the only two immortals not plied with gifts and prayers. (ll. 166-9)

Where does interpretation begin? Why is there such a thing at all? In the story of Hermes, interpretation begins in impatience with the given, in restlessness, and in hunger. There are other choices besides interpretation, certainly. There is repetition: you repeat what has gone before, accept its authority, carry the past forward, place the present under the sign of the past, or tell the story of the present and future as the known story which comes from the past. One repeats sometimes out of love, sometimes out of self-interest, sometimes fear, sometimes faith, sometimes conviction, and sometimes because there seems to be nothing else to do.

There is the choice of silence: say nothing, tell no story, put no question. One is silent sometimes out of a willingness for others to tell and decide, sometimes out of confusion, sometimes out of fear of speaking or being heard—fear of being confronted in the uncertainty of dialogue. Sometimes one is silent out of resistance or rebellion—silent in order to be free, at least in the sanctuary of an imagination which is different from what is repeated.

There is the choice of telling a new story: you place a new story alongside or over against what is repeated, you make a claim upon the present from a different direction. Tell a story from a different past than the one which has been repeated, or tell a story from the future, and talk of what is beginning rather than returning. Sometimes it is told because there is nothing to lose, since the past and present are times of loss already. Sometimes it is because there is something to gain, a horizon, a vision. Sometimes it is out of boredom with repeating, and any story is better than one which is boring.

Interpretation is not the only choice, then, and what distinguishes it from repetition, silence, or novelty is not the dissatisfaction, restlessness, or hunger, but its double vision. It looks toward the future, but talks about the past; it dwells upon what is repeated, but in order to point away from it. Interpretation is rooted in the "textual" nature of human experience. That is, it is rooted in the gathering of human experience into stable and repeatable narratives, patterns, and relationships by which human beings (individually and together) represent their world to themselves. Such "textual" reality, because of its stable and repeated nature, always has the quality of the past to it. One *interprets* because of the unavoidable presence of the past; one *interprets* for the sake of the future; one *interprets* in order to shape the story of the future by reshaping the story of the past.

Interpretation, viewed through the lens of this myth, is founded upon hunger. Hermes is hungry. He declares that he and his mother have been wrongfully kept apart from the community of the gods, which is true (ll. 165-81). They are kept apart because of the perpetual conflict between Zeus and Hera, and because he and Maia—his very birth itself—are signs of the conflict. They are signs of the wrong which the most powerful gods have done to each other. They are signs of how that wrong is played out upon the lives of those who are less powerful. Simply because their presence is a testimony, they must be kept apart. Hermes vows to do what he must, whatever that may be, for them to stand where they belong.

Interpretation under the sign of Hermes begins in desire. Whether or not the desire has a just claim on an ultimate scale does not matter. We are in the more elemental realm of hunger and need, the realm of root questions about what it means to be a living being among other living beings: to eat, to have a place, to have power within your own life, to belong, to speak and be heard. We are in a realm where equations of pure power are the calculations which matter. What one needs is not to be *justified*, as if there were some court of appeal outside the gods to which one could turn with a claim which has some force because of its inherent justice. The ones who judge are the very one's whose power and conflict, whose warfare, has been written onto the bodies of the less powerful; and there is no Judge who can judge the judges. What one needs is not to be argued, but *secured*.

> And if my father does not allow me this, I shall surely
> try to be, as I no doubt can, the chief of robbers.
> And if [Apollo] seeks to find me,
> then I think he will meet with some greater loss.
> For to Pytho I shall go and break my way into his great house,
> whence many beautiful tripods and cauldrons

I shall plunder, and gold, too, and gleaming iron
and many garments. (ll. 174-81)

When the desire for a different future takes the path of
interpretation it enters the realm of speech, and there it is
transformed into desire for a *hearing*. To speak and be heard
becomes a sign for those other fundamental needs, just as being
silenced or refused a hearing becomes a sign of their deprivation. Speech is, among other things, a claim of power, worth,
position, a right to be heard. Speech happens in a dynamic of
giving and receiving, withholding and taking, an economy of
privilege and poverty.

Not every voice, after all, can claim the hearing that it wants
or needs. There is always other speech to contend with, a cho-
rus of voices among which one must be heard, for the hunger
is everywhere. The voices compete in whatever space is allowed
them (or taken by them) within the hierarchy of speech. There
are, indeed, such established hierarchies; there is speech or
texts which have prior claim to hearing, whose claim excludes,
resists, or allows a hearing on its own terms for new speech.
The speech of the gods, oracles, and sacred texts make the
ultimate prior claim. That is part of what it *means* to call some
speech "sacred": to point to its priority, its power to shape
what will be said and who will say it. This is not necessarily
either negative or positive, coercive or liberating. The power of
a text to generate other texts may be liberating and yet still may
point to its own priority. A hearing, then, must be gained in the
arena of established speech, in connection with—but also over
against—the speech of another. At its greatest intensification the
struggle to speak happens in the arena enclosed by the speech
of the gods.

There are different ways to enter that arena, as we have
said, but interpretation enters through the taking up and taking
over of another's authoritative speech. Interpretation gains a
hearing through repetition of an established text, by pointing to
the past, the fixed, the stable. But it is only a partial repetition.
The concern is for the future, for a future different from the
repetition of the past. In taking up another's speech, therefore,
interpretation subverts the direction and purpose of the very

speech that gives it entry. Insofar as it is not repetition, it is subversion. No longer does interpretation serve to express the origin, the text; it serves instead as the way to a hearing for the interpreter. There is where the theft occurs. The text is a pre-text. Hermes steals Apollo's cattle, but not for their own sake, in order to consume them; he does not eat what he takes. Hermes steals them because through them he can achieve what he desires.

There would seem to be an ownership of words: not of language itself (quite the reverse), but of words which have been configured and domesticated by a particular person or group. Texts and speech may "belong." They stand under a particular name and are extensions of that name. They are representations of their owner and point to their owner as a sign of wealth and claim to hearing, and as a sign of being bound to their owner's will. The "ownership" of words means the right to exercise will over them, to say what they mean, how they will be used, in what sense, for what purpose, and by whom. Owned speech or texts appear to be dominated, then, by the will and intention of their owners. (Words, speech, and text, although they are quite different at certain levels of analysis, are used interchangeably here.) Owners are not necessarily authors, although they may be. A community of authoritative interpretation can be the owner. Even the idea of "meaning" itself can be the owner of a text, as when we say interpretation must be true to the "meaning of the text." The idea of a meaning which stands behind a text, to which one may appeal for a judgement, is part of this same economy.

Interpretation is founded upon displacing such ownership, revealing it as a fiction kept in place by *agreement*, rather than by some effective power. Texts are not bound to their origin, just as the cattle are not bound to theirs. Taking possession and privilege over them only makes visible what was true all along. It makes no difference that there may have been a commission, or an entrusting of the words to the one who uses them. The transition from receiving words given to keeping them for one's own is an internal one. It has to do with how the interpreter regards what has been given, the one to whom it now belongs, who now has authority to dispose of these words. Theft is an interior reality.

The theft that founds interpretation, however, must be disguised. It must be disguised because the situation of interpretation, which brings together text, interpreter, and hearer, is founded upon an *agreed fiction*. The fiction of interpretation depends upon concealing the fact that theft has happened and that there is no other owner of the words speaking through them. What makes it *interpretation* is the appeal to a figure who is absent and silent, unseen and unheard. The text, the speech, are displayed as remaining under the power and will of their originator, as is the interpreter, ostensibly. The words, like Apollo's cattle, appear to point in one direction, but their movement is, in fact, in another. They seem to point to their origin, but they are driven in another way, with the traces of who is guiding them distorted. That is a matter of invention and craft; Hermes is the father of both.

> And the old man replied to [Apollo] and said:
> "Friend, it is hard to tell all that one sees with his eyes;
> for so many are the wayfarers traveling this road,
> some of them bent on many evil things while others
> go after what is good, and no easy task it is to know each one.
> I thought I saw a child—I can't be sure.
> This child, an infant, too . . .
> drove [the cows] with tails backwards and heads facing toward
>   him." (ll. 201-5; 208-9, 11)

> [Hermes said] "I vow that I myself am not the culprit
> and that I have seen no one else stealing your cows . . . (ll. 275-6)
>   Surely I neither stole the cows . . . nor saw another do
> it. (ll. 275-6; 310-11)
>   Father Zeus, I, indeed, shall speak the truth to you,
> for I am all for the truth and know not how to lie." (ll. 368-9)

The lie is perhaps the sharpest and clearest deception within the world of our story, since it is speech about speech and undercuts all. "I vow that I am not the culprit . . . I shall speak the truth to you, for I am all for the truth and know not how to lie." The public vow of interpretation is a vow of loyalty to the text; that is, it claims to interpret *this* text or *that*. It claims to speak *about* this or that in a way which is somehow loyal—whether to the origin beyond the text, or to some intention within the text, or at the most basic level, to the simple order of words. In some cases the vow of loyalty even includes a denial that any interpretation is happening. This is the most subversive of vows. One interprets but claims only to repeat. That too is part of the fiction.

As with every deception, however, there is the possibility of witnesses, those who see and stand outside the deception. The witness sees a strange sight, and no wonder, for there is a fantastic quality to the scene of interpretation. In the "Hymn" there is the terrific clash of perceptions. There appears to be an infant, the very image of weakness, yet here he drives the cattle on, and strides back and forth across the road like a giant, while all the while the cattle are driven backwards. What is anyone to make of it? For even a god such as Apollo cannot decipher the story or the tracks. Although the witness is warned not to tell of the ruse that has occurred, the warning is hardly necessary, for he is *unable* to do so, except to say what he has seen, which makes no sense. In Ovid's variation (*Metamorphoses* 2.680-707) the position of the witness is most revealing. He promises Hermes to keep silent, but when the god returns in disguise to test him, he breaks the promise. For punishment Hermes turns him into a stone without sight, hearing, or speech.

Fiction makes a covenant, a covenant which says its partners agree to a shared "world" for a while. A fiction is a narrative construct, a framework for communication and understanding, which for a time is regarded as "real enough" for the purposes of those who create it and those who participate in it. It sets possibilities and limits, names the conditions under which one works and the problem at hand. It assigns roles to those who participate in it. This covenant (usually implicit) serves the same function as the presupposition of an argument, which provides a foundation upon which discourse may go forward. In the same way, a fiction about interpretation provides a framework or world in which interpretation takes place. The witness who betrays the fiction is left unable to see, speak, or hear, for apart from such a fiction (that one or another) there is no possibility for interpretation. That's what interpretation *is*: participation in the fiction, whether as interpreter or hearer.

36

Step outside the fiction and the cords which hold things together on a common ground are cut. The text slips away, and the (fictional) Judge disappears. There is nothing outside the immediate relationship of interpreter and hearer to which either may appeal. Both are returned to the pure equation of power where what matters is what one can secure. Step outside of the fiction of interpretation and there is chaos.[11]

In interpretation the interpreter and hearer agree to a story about what they are doing together. It is a story about a gift of meaning, where it comes from, and how it comes. In this story, meaning is to be found in the speech or texts of an absent other, but that meaning must be communicated by an interpreter who guarantees that it really is the "other's" gift which has been given. Meaning stands over against both parties as the object of desire which makes the story happen. It is to be given or withheld, lost or found, taken or retaken, hidden or revealed, to name but a few possibilities. Each one is founded upon the story of origins one tells, that is, the story of how there came to be such a lack in the first place. "Once there was . . . and then . . . and now . . . therefore, we . . . so you." The possibility of meaning is framed by a fiction, and interpretation plays out the various plots which that fiction's world allows. In order to approach meaning, or to have the experience of meaning approaching me, I enter into this fiction about where meaning is found—a fiction which I know at some level of myself *is* a fiction.

This is more than a fiction one reads, however; it is a fiction one *enacts*. That is, the interpreter and the hearer *perform* this as a drama, as theater. The "world" is not only a place of imagination and possibilities; it is also a place of action. The story of the desire for meaning is performed episode after episode, scene after scene. It may be truer, in this light, to say that experience has a *dramatic* quality rather than a narrative quality. It is told, on the one hand, as a narrative which was first of all enacted; it is enacted, on the other hand, as the performance of what has been told. The recognition of interpretation as theater makes the interpretive fiction that much more visible. Even the false interpreter, therefore, is not an enemy to meaning as such, but necessary to the story of it and the drama of it. The false interpreter becomes a character in the plot, a fictional enemy playing out original possibilities. Although Hermes knows he is lying, he appeals to Zeus to judge the truth. Why? For the sake of the fiction. The real enemy of it all is chaos; that is, the destruction of the story and its enactment.

Interpretation under the sign of the herald, then, is performance, drama. As theater, the drama of interpretation is governed by the same willingness to see and not to see that all theater demands. We agree that the stage is a certain place, the time a certain time, the players not themselves but others, because we are offered an experience of meaning in exchange. Quite apart from the content of interpretation, speaker and hearer enact a drama of hidden characters sending messages, mediators carrying them across boundaries and dangers (which may include the mediators themselves), and receivers for whom the message supplies their lack.[12] Regardless of the particular content, one could argue, *that* is the story, the drama, the theater which is being enacted in interpretation.

Interpretation is thus a work of deception carried out by impostors in front of those who know that they are impostors but who are willing to be deceived. Why? For the sake of meaning. Interpretation is the drama of meaning, its meeting place and meeting time. The experience of meaning is an experience of meeting, as Buber might say. It is an experience contained within a ritual drama about exactly that: how there is such a wonderful thing as meaning, how it came to be, and how it has reached all the way to here, where we have gathered.

It must be remembered, however, that this is a theater of the fantastic, the uncanny, and the marvelous. There are charms, curses, miraculous transports, and changes of form; an infant who speaks, who strides like a giant, who can change into a mist, who can even charm gods with mysterious music. The terms "fantastic," "uncanny," and "marvelous" are intended in particular ways. Tzvetan Todorov, in his study of the literary genre of the fantastic (1973), describes the heart of the fantastic as a *hesitation*. One is confronted by an event which defies the immediate laws of the world one knows. The choice is forced: Is it illusion, perhaps, or imagination? Or is the world subject to laws hitherto unknown? "The fantastic occupies the duration of this uncertainty. Once we choose one answer or the other, we leave the fantastic for a neighboring genre, the uncanny or the marvelous. The fantastic is that hesitation experienced by a person who knows only the laws of nature, confronting an apparently supernatural event" (Todorov 1973:25).

The uncanny may be distinguished from the fantastic as the "fantastic-explained." That is, the hesitation is resolved by deciding that it is imagination or illusion at work, subject to an explanation within the laws of the world one has inhabited all along. The events were a dream, let us say, or the work of a drug, or of hidden agents now revealed. The marvelous may be called the "fantastic-accepted." The hesitation is resolved by deciding that there is a different world at hand which operates according to its own laws. The events were the work of angels or devils, let us say, or of gods one had not known, with powers one had never before seen (Todorov 1973:41-57).

The fantastic begins, then, in the unsettling of perception, and endures as long as the multiple possibilities remain open. It is essentially dynamic, dialectical, unstable. It both provokes a desire for resolution and thwarts the desire it provokes. The deeper the tension between its uncanny and marvelous transformations, the deeper the desire it provokes for both kinds of resolution; or the deeper the desire for only one kind (because the other is so terrible to contemplate, let us say, and therefore fascinating), the more fantastic it is.

Within his own story Hermes is sometimes fantastic (as when he is witnessed by the farmer), sometimes uncanny (as when he makes strange sandals to cover his tracks), and sometimes marvelous (as when he changes shapes into a mist). Interpretation under his sign is thus a theater of all three. It begins in the creation of uncertainty, pressing upon the hearer as a crisis of perception. The crisis has to do with what is fixed and what is open, what is real and what is illusory, what is powerful and effective and what is not, what is "past and passing and to come," to borrow from Yeats. Through this lure of the fantastic, interpretation draws attention to itself and holds out the desirability and possibility of a resolution which it may either deny or provide according to the interpreter's special knowledge of the origin, the source of meaning. The hearer may be shown that the uncertainty was finally nothing more than uncanny, a misunderstanding. The answer was here in the "text" all along; all that was needed was to read more closely. Or the hearer may be shown that the reason for uncertainty is that one has misperceived the source in a fundamental way. It never was what one supposed it to be, but has been something else all along, and the hearer, therefore, has been living in unreality. To understand, the hearer must accept the marvelous new world of the "text," which the interpreter reveals.

There are other aspects of the "Hymn" which gather around the images we have considered here: the engagement with Apollo, the exchange of the cattle for the lyre, Apollo's refusal to give the power of divination, and more. They all may be read into a continuous story of the situation of interpretation, configured under the sign of Hermes. Let this be enough for now, so we may gather things together to see what they make.

Under the sign of Hermes interpretation we discover a magic theater of desire performed at the place where boundaries meet: the past and present, present and future, inclusion and exclusion, the fixed and the open, poverty and wealth, privileged speech and unprivileged speech, fiction and chaos, the seeming and the real, lie and truth, possible and impossible, living and dead, wild and tame, music which means without saying and speech which says without meaning, one person and another, what I have done and what I will do. That is, it is a theater of desire—hungry for a different future, which does not transmit, but transforms—performed at the place where the gods and humankind meet.

WHERE INTERPRETATION BEGINS

In the preceding pages the task has been to think about the nature of interpretation through the configured oppositions of a certain myth. The question of whether or not, and in what ways, one believes any of it to be true has been put aside for a time in order to develop the thickness of the myth's world and the forces at work within it.

This is not a story to which I am bound, in the way I am bound to Scripture, for example, or to certain traditions of interpretation. That is to say, it has no authority in principle for me, no prior claim to a hearing or to accountability. Whatever authority it has comes only from recognition: whether and how one recognizes oneself as interpreter, and one's interpretative situation in the contradictions of Hermes. What does it mean, then, to be open to such a text and where it leads? It means to let the questions it raises be taken up as questions put to us. There are any number of questions one might take up, but there is one from which all the others emerge: the question of desire.

The myth of Hermes presses the question of the desire which lies at the heart of interpretation. If interpretation is founded upon desire, then that desire, or the dynamic of desire itself, informs everything which follows. Call it a search, or call it hunger; call it lack, or exclusion, or deprivation. Those are terms of absence, of course, but the question can and should be put positively as well. What is the hope, the vision, the commitment, the dream? What is the *future* that one's interpretation seeks? What is the desire?

In Hermes the question is pressed at an elemental level. It is one thing for any of us to answer for the particular guild we serve. That is easy enough and may be done "correctly" and with the proper warrants, which is to say, without a certain kind of risk. It is another to answer as the particular individual one is. In Hermes we meet the questions of our own anger and our own love, our own sense of violation, loss, and estrangement. In Hermes we meet the questions of relationship and place. With whom are we in relationship, and where does this relationship happen? Who are the people to whom we have particular loyalty, and for whom we act? Hermes acted on behalf of himself and Maia. On whose behalf do you and I act? In one sense, Hermes presents the challenge of an elemental honesty. It is a challenge to name one's person, place, and commitments at what some might call the simplest level (or what others might call the most fundamental), and to recognize that the work of interpretation originates there.

To translate into the language of my own religious tradition, this is to say that interpretation is founded upon confession. It is a twofold confession: the confession of who I am, and the confession of what I believe. Eventually the confession must turn to a story of interpretation in the same way: a story of what it is, and a story of what I want it to be. If it is, in fact, a confession of sin and faith, then such stories end in a prayer. A prayer that the Name be holy, God's realm come, and God's will be done; a prayer that our daily hunger be fed, our sin forgiven, and our lives not be brought to the dreadful test.

I confess that I am a thief of Another's words, who distorts them and erases them, lies about it, and breaks oaths. I confess that this is what an interpreter does, and an interpreter is what I have chosen to be. I confess than mine is an exegesis of desire by which I hope to gain a life for myself and others—some of whom I know, most of whom I do not. I confess that I am an imposter who plays a part in a fantastic drama.

I confess, therefore, that the story of Hermes is my story, but it is not my only story. The passion of interpretation is deeper than any one story can fathom, and story gives way to story as depths darken into depths. So there are other stories of interpretation to tell, and stories beyond those, and still more stories. What I pray is this: although I am an impostor, God grant that I may nevertheless be one of the "impostors who speaks the truth."

3

THE
EXEGESIS
OF
TEARS

t is recounted in the Talmud that one day, Rabbi Eliezar and the Sages (that is, the other Rabbis) were disputing over the ritual purity of a certain oven. The debate was fierce, and the Sages "encompassed [the oven] with words as a snake" to prove it unclean.

> It has been taught: On that day R. Eliezar brought forward every imaginable argument, but they did not accept them. Said he to them: "If the halachah [legal teaching] agrees with me, let this carob-tree prove it!" Thereupon the carob-tree was torn a hundred cubits out of its place—others affirm, four hundred cubits. "No proof can be brought from a carob-tree," they retorted.
>
> Again he said to them: "If the halachah agrees with me, let the stream of water prove it!" Whereupon the stream of water flowed backwards. "No proof can be brought from a stream of water," they rejoined.
>
> Again he urged, "If the halachah agrees with me, let the walls of the schoolhouse prove it," whereupon the walls inclined to fall. But R. Joshua rebuked them, saying, "When scholars are engaged in a halachic dispute, what have ye to interfere?" Hence they did not fall, in honor of R. Joshua, nor did they resume the upright, in honor of R. Eliezar; and they are still standing thus inclined.
>
> Again he said to them: "If the halachah agrees with me,

let it be proved from Heaven!" Whereupon a Heavenly Voice cried out: "Why do ye dispute with R. Eliezar, seeing that in all matters the halachah agrees with him!" But R. Joshua arose and exclaimed: "IT IS NOT IN HEAVEN" (Deut 30:12). What did he mean by this? Said R. Jeremiah: "That the Torah had already been given at Mount Sinai; we pay no attention to a Heavenly Voice, because Thou hast long since written in the Torah at Mount Sinai, AFTER THE MAJORITY MUST ONE INCLINE (Ex 23:2).

R. Nathan met Elijah and asked him: "What did the Holy One, Blessed be He, do in the hour?" "He laughed [with joy]," he replied, "saying, 'My sons have defeated me, My sons have defeated me.'" (Baba Mezi'a 59b)[1]

This is a story about interpretation in crisis. It is a story about much else, as well: authority, community, reason, signs, traces, heavenly voice, God, laughter, holiness, law, words. All of this is only to say once again that it is a story of interpretation in crisis, for such a crisis is never simple. Although the crisis comes from a time and tradition far distant, its features are well known to us now; every crisis of interpretation is in some ways the same. Take any of these themes and there is enough to occupy a lifetime; take all of them together and who can find a way through? Perhaps it is only in a story that the horizons, the dimensions, of such a crisis can be seen together.

Yet even to see this one story whole it is necessary to see others, too. Every story of a crisis—if it is a real crisis, one which grows from deep authentic dimensions of the community itself—rests upon a prior story. There may be a story of beginnings which tells how the crisis began in the very first things, perhaps how it was even intended or inevitable. There may be a story of the present, one which tells why such a crisis matters to anyone enough to turn toward an old story for help. There may be a story of the future one hopes for or fears, a story which is imagined but not yet enacted, because of which such a story as ours is brought forward. Prior does not necessarily mean a priority in time; it means a priority of world.

It is one thing to tell a story about Hermes and the Greek gods, and the place of interpretation. It is quite another thing to tell a story about the one Israel calls the LORD. Those gods

44

themselves are very different from the god of Israel, to be sure: very different characters in a very different story. Most important of all, there is no comparable scripture, no authoritative canon which is set in story itself as the place where the LORD may be met.

The issue of the authority of sacred texts and their authoritative interpretation is, of course, at the very heart of both the Jewish and Christian story. Whoever else Jesus was, he was an interpreter of sacred texts, in a long and dynamic tradition of interpretation. Whoever else Paul was, he too was an interpreter of sacred texts, and heir to the methods and ethos of rabbinic tradition.[2] Although rabbinic literature seems foreign to most Christians, we may be more acquainted with it than we know. Most of our biblical texts, it has been argued, are themselves products of the world of rabbinic interpretation. Whenever we turn to our scriptures we wade into a stream flowing from that world, however aware or unaware one may be of the source. There are other tributaries to that stream, of course, flowing from other sources, more familiar, closer. But their concerns could hardly be more central to the church than those of the ancient Rabbis. The word of God and the interpretation of the community for its own time, those questions which are so vital and troublesome to the church now, are the very essence of rabbinic Judaism. These are ancient forbears whose struggles carry striking resemblances to those of our time.

SITTING WITH THE RABBIS

There is a picture, perhaps only in my imagination, of ancient rabbis sitting together, the Book open before them. They may be enemies, they may be friends, they may be strangers, but what matters is that they belong to the Book, and through the Book they belong together. The Book is the world and the world is the Book; to live is to interpret, and to interpret is to live. But they can only do it together, not alone. To approach our story of Eliezar and the Sages, we must begin with the foundations of the story in the world of rabbinic interpretation.

A common term in rabbinic interpretation is "midrash." The word is built upon a root which means "to search" or "to search out."[3] It may be applied to study and public interpretation of the Bible or other sacred texts in Judaism, such as the Mishnah (the compilation of the Oral Torah) and the Gemara (the commentary upon the Mishnah, which together comprise the Talmud). As is so often true of words in Hebrew, "midrash" has multiple possibilities and meanings. It can mean an actual interpretation of a portion of scripture. One opens the Book, reads, and says what the scripture means. Midrash may also be a compilation of such interpretations, a collection of "midrashim." As there is a Book, there are also Books of the Book which are just as important. But midrash also is the process of interpretation itself, the "searching out" of meaning for the text (Neusner 1987:9). Interpretation is a search; interpreters are searchers; what must be found is meaning.

What are those ancient companions doing as they sit together there in the house of study? They are searching, exploring, voyaging, from before the foundations of the earth to the world to come, from the heart of the page to the heart of the universe. For what are they searching? For meaning.

TEXT IN SEARCH OF INTERPRETATION: COMMUNITY, DIALOGUE, OPENNESS

Midrash is a process, a way of life, more than a method. There are methods within the process, to be sure; there are rules and models and techniques which are applied. But the process is larger than the execution of techniques. It entails dynamic relationships between God and text, text and text, text and interpreter, interpreter and interpreter, God and community, community and history, text and history, text and creation. The process has been described by Gerald Bruns (1987:636) as "exemplary of all interpretation that is open to the historicality of human life," a process that lives in the full flow and flux of history, surrendering neither past nor present and fully accountable to both, which teaches about "all interpretation, whatever the method, when 'interpretation' *matters* to human life" (632).

The heart of midrash is found in the relationship between authoritative text and authoritative interpretation.[4] There is not one Torah, but two. One is written, one is oral, but both are

46

given by God at Sinai, and both are divine. In the written Torah God has given and intended all; everything is filled with intention and meaning, and always there is more. Letters, numbers, shapes, omissions, repetitions, unusual forms of words, anagrams—nothing is there by accident. Even God is a student of the Torah, and turned to the Torah to find the blueprint for creation. "To understand creation one looks not to nature but to the Torah; the world can be read out of the Torah, and the Torah read from the world" (Handelman 1982: 38). Interpretation is essential, therefore, because it is the unlocking of the richness given in the Book but awaiting disclosure at the necessary time and place.

Midrash is the reaching out of Scripture itself. The Torah is given. But, as the tradition goes, all its future interpretation is foreseen and given, too—not subsequent to Torah, but alongside, and that interpretation is Torah also. The two Torahs are given at once, but as letters must unfold and be read in sequence, so too the interpretation can only unfold through time and community.

The face of the Scriptures is turned toward its future rather than its past. The text desires and even demands interpretation. The Bible claims, intends, seeks, reaches. It is subject, more than object. Torah is a sort of living being that means and intends as a living being. Interpretation is the living voice of that living being. It is with the time of interpretation that the Scriptures are chiefly concerned; they cast their light ahead of them, toward understanding, appropriation, into an ongoing revelation to be taken up into the concrete and specific acts and language of a community.[5] For the scriptures *bind* as well as *mean*. They bind the community which interprets them to ways of being in its own time, and they bind the community to the Scriptures themselves. The medium through which the Bible does this is interpretation, midrash.

The context of interpretation is community. One studies and interprets in community and as community. What one studies is community also. The midrashist who studies scripture studies a community of texts; the midrashist who studies midrash studies a community of speech. Regardless of the particular words on the page, the form of the writings themselves are community, and that community is a communion of interpretation. The process is dialogue. One voice, then another, then another. If it is halachia, a matter of law, there will be a ruling, but all the dissenting voices will remain. They remain because without them the ruling could never have been tested and refined. They remain because they are themselves authoritative. There is a famous story of a dispute between the Houses of Hillel and Shammai. After they could reach no agreement, at last a voice came from Heaven saying, "the law is according to Hillel, but both of them are the words of the living God" (TJ Ber.1:7, 3b). Whatever force, whatever meaning authority has, it is one that proceeds from the dialogue itself.

The story of midrash, then, is founded upon the conviction that the text in all its parts is divine, potent, inexhaustible, seeking and intending and teaching its own interpretation through a process which is foreseen by God but can only unfold through the free, imaginative, and disciplined play of the community. The implications of such a picture of interpretation are vast, indeed. The voice of God, the words of scripture, and the interpretation of the community are drawn into a relationship, into a process, into a life, which is at once delicate and dynamic, complementary and clashing.

Let us return to the story of Eliezar and see what story of interpretation it has to tell. Let us ask about the task of interpretation itself as we face it, as we sift among the words of scripture, the voice of God, and the voices of the community, to discover what the Rabbis may disclose to us about our own interpretive situation in all its possibility and danger.

THE OVEN OF 'AKNAI

R. Eliezar declared it clean, and the Sages declared it unclean; and this was the oven of 'Aknai. Why 'Aknai? Said Rab Judah in Samuel's name: [It means] that they encompassed it with arguments [literally, words] as a snake. It has been taught: On that day R. Eliezar brought forward every imaginable argument [literally, every argument in the world], but they did not accept them.

The oven of 'Aknai is encompassed with words, encompassed as by a snake (which the name may also mean). Whatever else the oven may be, including clean or unclean, it is named after this: its reality is wrapped in words. What it will be to the community, what effect it will have upon people and things, what the response of the community to it must be—all this will be determined by the oven's relationship to words. Words prove. Prove means to demonstrate, but also to test, and that is the older sense. The oven is ringed and proved. Eliezar, however, brings "every argument in the world." If he has brought all argument, then what have the Sages brought? They have the proof. So what is this relationship between the two? What does proof prove? How does proof convince? What counts as proof? Maybe proof is a closed system unto itself. Maybe proof proves nothing about anything except the community that accepts it. The language of proof is one thing, the language of declaration another. In the world of declaration, proof establishes nothing. Declaration is what makes it so. Proof is not executed; verdicts are.

The oven is not the issue. The Scriptures are not the issue, nor is purity. The issue is the authority to interpret. The issue is the shape of interpretive authority within the community, which means the shape of the community itself. Arguments, even all the arguments in the world, mean little compared to the power to name, declare, and enforce, to say what is true and to bind acts upon the community that enforce the authority of the declared truth. But surely there must be some limit to our power to declare and have it be. Only God speaks and it comes to pass. So what is it that comes to pass when the community speaks? And what is the limit?

> Said [Eliezar] to them: "If the halachah agrees with me, let this carob-tree prove it!" Thereupon the carob-tree was torn a hundred cubits out of its place--others affirm, four hundred cubits. "No proof can be brought from a carob-tree," they retorted.

If not arguments, then let there be signs. There will be a test. Eliezar calls the carob-tree as a witness. A prophet can declare such a test; Elijah did on Mt. Carmel (1 Kgs 18:36-38).

A prophet can call upon a sign to demonstrate where the truth lies, because there is a guarantor who stands behind the prophet's words. Prophets may turn from argument and declare, "Thus says the LORD," and if it is a true prophet, it will come to pass. Is Eliezar a prophet? Who speaks for God?

But the Sages have asked for no such test. They have demanded nothing beyond the testing of interpretation by interpretation. Words are a world unto themselves. They point to themselves. Signs are a world unto themselves, too. The place where language and signs clash is confused. Like wind and tide moving obliquely or in opposite directions, the surface heaps up, the edges of waves break into spray, and the division between air and water is blurred. The broken zone between two fluid orders of words and signs is where the interpreter works, struggling to read them both and make a way.

What could the testimony Eliezar demands prove, anyway? To whom is the issue so important that this miraculous witness should be summoned? For the sake of an oven does one call upon miracles of nature? But then the oven is not the issue, and neither is the law the issue. Who will interpret, and who will say which interpretation is binding? For this perhaps one may justly call for a miracle, because so much is at stake.

"No proof may be brought from a carob-tree," the Sages respond. True enough. If all the arguments of the world are not sufficient, then what *more* does a carob-tree have to say? It is a sign to the one who asks for it, but no-sign to those who do not. The tree may tell the truth, or the tree may be a liar; it makes no difference. Worse than ambiguous, it is irrelevant. Signs are signs only among other signs. As we shall see, signs clash and cancel one another, and speak only to their own loyalists. But this sign may be troubling, nonetheless. Root, branch, shoot, stump, flower, a tree torn from its place and thrown far, some say farther—why *this* sign? Perhaps this is a warning of what is to come, or an enactment of what already is; no one will interpret or say. There is something ominous in this sign. But then, there is something ominous in *every* sign. The sheer fact of a sign is ominous. It hints of another order, another power, another judgment.

Says Eliezar, "If the halachah agrees with me, let the stream of water prove it!" Whereupon the stream of water flowed backwards. "No proof can be brought from a stream of water," they rejoined.

Surely this would give one pause. An uprooted tree is one thing, wonderful to be sure, but in the world of signs it is uncertain. And we have seen a stream of water reversing its course before. At the Red Sea it happened once, so the people could cross over from Egypt to the wilderness—where they would receive the law and wander. At the Jordan it happened once, so the people could cross over from wandering into the promised land. What makes water reverse its course?

> The sea looked and fled,
> Jordan turned back . . .
> What ails you, O sea, that you flee?
> O Jordan, that you turn back?
> . . . Tremble, O earth, at the presence
> of the LORD. (Ps 114:3, 5, 7)

Presence makes water change its course, it would seem. Signs testify to presence. Eliezar is neither Joshua nor Moses. Nevertheless, he commands streams of water; he commands streams of water, but he cannot command the Sages. This sign is more ominous than the last.

> "Let the walls of the schoolhouse prove it," whereupon the walls inclined to fall. But R. Joshua rebuked them, saying: "When scholars are engaged in a halachic dispute, what have ye to interfere?" Hence they did not fall, in honour of R. Joshua, nor did they resume the upright, in honour of R. Eliezar; and they are still standing thus inclined.

Here is another sign. But this time R. Joshua commands signs as well. The wall inclines to fall but is rebuked. The clash is fully open now: word against word, sign against sign. Aaron and the magicians of Pharaoh's court once dueled in such a way. Aaron gave his sign, the magicians gave theirs; then the signs themselves fought, and signs swallowed up signs (Exod 7:11-13). That, too, was a battle of snakes. But there the clash remained opaque and unreadable.

The schoolhouse wall can neither straighten nor fall. The *school*house wall . . . If it falls it must be rebuilt; a new school would appear. If it straightens back, there is no need. Everything is in place and everything may proceed. Interpretation may proceed, the work of words may proceed. Neither fallen nor straight, the walls "are still standing thus inclined." Still. The sign remains. Go, look, read, and tell us what testimony these walls have to give.

The impasse has been reached. Arguments have proven no proof. Signs collide and testify too little or too much or too differently to matter. What is left to bridge between the two, or better yet, to stand over both? There must be something that is unambiguous and sovereign in the realm of words and the realm of signs both. There must be a word that speaks with the presence of a sign and a sign that speaks with the declaration of words.

"Let it be proved from Heaven!"

The fullness of the crisis has come. The appeal has been made for a ruling once and for all. The request itself is troubling. For whose sake is it made? For Israel's sake? But if Eliezar could call upon a heavenly voice, then why wait for this matter of an oven? Perhaps it is for the Sages' sake, to teach them. But to teach them what? About halachah? About proof? About themselves? About heaven? About Eliezar? Perhaps the request is simply for the sake of Eliezar, for his wound, his rejection, for vindication.

The voice, however, gives more than is asked. One ruling is all that is requested; what is given amounts to the unveiling of a second Moses: "Why do you dispute with R. Eliezar, seeing that in all matters the halachah agrees with him!"

All matters? This is too much. Too much is at stake. To follow this voice means interpretation is at an end. The Book is closed, the world is closed, the Word is closed. To follow this voice means the Book is not infinite, infinitely capable, inexhaustible, encompassing every other book. It is, instead, a book among books, holy but not Holy. And if the Book has such a limit, is God not limited also? Did the God who studied Torah in order to create the world study a finite thing among other things? With this the community of interpretation is at an end, as well. If the halachah agrees with Eliezer in all matters, what need is there for a people? What dialogue is necessary, or even possible, between God and Israel or Israel and Israel? If the Book is closed, its language is brittle not elastic, and what is brittle breaks without disclosing. Too much is at stake to listen to a voice from Heaven saying this. For the sake of Heaven, then, one must not listen to Heaven.

R. Joshua arose and exclaimed, "IT IS NOT IN HEAVEN."

A voice from Heaven speaks. How shall one answer? A voice from Heaven speaks in a way that threatens everything, including Heaven itself. R. Joshua answers with Torah, citing Scripture against Heaven for the sake of Heaven, earth, and Israel:

> For this commandment which I command you this day is not too hard for you, neither is it far off. It is not in heaven, that you should say, "Who will go up for us to heaven, and bring it to us, that we may hear it and do it?" . . . But the word is very near you; it is in your mouth and in your heart, so that you can do it. (Deut 30:11-12, 14)

The story has come to its highest point in this opposition between the Heavenly Voice and the text of Torah. Eliezar fades from the story. The interpreter who can bring forward every argument in the world, the interpreter-prophet who can command both signs in nature and the Voice of Heaven, is eclipsed by R. Joshua, whose speech overshadows everything else. Who is the protagonist now?

There is a quality of shock to this climax. The logic of what precedes it does not demand that things turn out this way. It is within the climax itself that R. Joshua's words become, if not inevitable, at least necessary. But what is this shock (assuming that the reader is shocked)? Perhaps it is the nakedness with which the Rabbi lays bare the situation of all who interpret writings, sacred or otherwise.

The longing for a divine voice, the longing for some sovereign word or sign that will give to both their respective worlds an order which is not simply arbitrary but ultimately true—this is a powerful longing. To have such a longing, and then to read a story in which precisely that hunger is fulfilled! To find it fulfilled, but then have it rejected!

But R. Joshua is telling the truth, and that is the shock: not the rejection of the divine voice, but the recognition that R. Joshua is saying only what is most basic about all our interpretation. Of course we must work with only the voices at hand, the human voices of a human world. Even when the words belong to sacred scripture, they are still human words, to be read the only way we know: humanly. Why the conceit of loyalty to a Heavenly Voice I have never heard? How does that conceit serve except to obscure my responsibility in a fantasy of interpretive rescue and certainty? The voice of God, R. Joshua says in so many words, is not a voice from Heaven. It is the voice of the community as it struggles together to read and interpret.

As the story reaches this height, I lose my bearings. Whose side am I on here? Has it changed? Where am I?

> What did he mean by this? Said R. Jeremiah: "That the Torah had already been given at Mount Sinai; we pay no attention to a Heavenly Voice, because Thou hast long since written in the Torah at Mount Sinai, "AFTER THE MAJORITY MUST ONE INCLINE" (Ex 23:2).

With this the story begins to close. The words of Scripture are vindicated. Interpretation is saved and the place of the interpretive community is secured. All that remains is a final turn to shape the reader's view of the story as a whole. Thus Elijah appears to one of the Rabbis, and upon questioning reports how God—far from being angry at the rejection of the Voice—laughed with joy, "My sons have defeated Me, My sons have defeated Me."

So this story appears to end happily. For all the seriousness, for all that was at stake, it is laughter, that claims the last word. If we have arrived at a place where God laughs with joy at the human insistence upon the responsibility to interpret, even at the cost of God's authority, then this must be a good place. The Sages, R. Joshua and the rest must have been right.

Now I am no Rabbi, but I have learned enough from listening to know that a rabbinic mind, even at the end of this story

54

might see a cloud passing across the face of the sun. If we pay no attention to a voice from Heaven, then why believe the report of Elijah? Why does this voice end the story, when it was not sufficient before? Why credit it now? Perhaps as a reader I believe it because I want to believe. I want to believe that Joshua is right, and I want the story to have a happy ending. But then I am still a believer in Heavenly Voices, one who has missed the weight of the story altogether.

Why does God say, "My sons have defeated Me" twice? That is another "rabbinic" kind of question. Perhaps there were two defeats. And if one defeat were good and joyful, the reasoning might go, then perhaps the other defeat was not joyful at all. The story may not be over.

THE WRONG OF WORDS,
THE CRIES OF THE WRONGED

The story of Eliezar and Joshua, as we have said, is a famous story. It is such a powerful and disturbing story that it stands on its own, certainly. But just what is the broader Talmudic conversation all about that it would take such a direction? We turn, therefore, to Baba Mezi'a of the Babylonian Talmud to read.

Baba Mezi'a, in which our story appears, is a tractate concerned principally with damages. It is full of the world of trade and industry, transactions, property lost and found, lending and credit, employers and employees. It is also concerned in great part with the problem of overreaching, that is, charging or paying too much. It is this last discussion that is underway as one comes close to the story of Eliezar and Joshua. For several portions of the Mishnah (the Oral Torah upon which the Gemara comments) various aspects of the problem of overreaching are addressed: how much is too much, what recourse one has, what sorts of goods or property are not subject to such restrictions, and so on. Then the Mishnah reads:

> Just as there is overreaching in buying and selling, so there is wrong done by words. One must not ask another, "What is the price of this article?" if he has no intention of buying. If a man was a repentant [sinner], one must not say to him, "Remember your former deeds." If he was a son of proselytes

one must not taunt him, "Remember the deeds of your ancestors," because it is written, THOU SHALT NEITHER WRONG A STRANGER, NOR OPPRESS HIM. (B.M. 58b)

There is a wrong done by words in the same way that there is a wrong done by charging or paying too much for goods. One may ask too much, one may value too much. One may misrepresent value or need, and step outside of some kind of true value, step outside of justice. This may happen, the Mishnah seems to say, in transactions of words as well as money.

The discussion of the Gemara which unfolds is too lengthy to reproduce here, but it is important to sketch the flow and note several important moments.

Initially, the commentary is content with a simple restatement of the Mishnah in slightly amplified form, adding examples and supporting citations. Then R. Johanan pushes the question farther: "Verbal wrong is more heinous than monetary wrong." To this another Rabbi adds, "The one affects the victim's person, the other only the victim's money."

The conversation escalates quickly then, with R. Nachman teaching, "The one who publicly shames [literally, makes pale] the neighbor is as though he shed blood." That is, when a person is shamed the blood drains from the face, and so is the same as the shedding of blood. Another teacher adds that the Jews of Palestine avoid this above all else, while still another insists it is so serious that the shaming of the neighbor is one of three offenses that deny a person a portion in the world to come. Stories then are brought forward to illustrate the seriousness of the offense. One Rabbi offers a reading that warns "Wrong not a people that is with you in learning and good deeds." So far, the themes have centered upon wrong done by words, shaming, loss of life, and concern for those who are part of the community of learning. In the next commentaries a new theme is introduced, one that will become critically important to Eliezar and the Sages: the theme of tears.

Since the destruction of the Temple, the gates of prayer are locked, for it is written, ALSO WHEN I CRY OUT, HE SHUTTETH OUT MY PRAYER. Yet though the gates of prayer are locked, the gates of tears are not. . . .

Another Rabbi teaches,

> All gates are locked, excepting the gates [through which pass the cries of] wrong, for it is written, BEHOLD THE LORD STOOD BY A WALL OF WRONGS, AND IN HIS HAND WERE THE WRONGS.

Then after several admonitions concerning the avoidance of strife in a household, related presumably to the power of tears, our story of Eliezar, the Sages, and the oven of 'Aknai appears.

In light of only the material which precedes it, the story would have several new dimensions of meaning to pursue. What is overreaching in words? What might it mean to value words too much? Who has overreached? Was it Eliezar or the Sages, or could it even be the Heavenly Voice? Even with only the questions arising from the Rabbinic commentary we have cited the shape of the story takes on difficult and important new edges for interpretation.

The story in the Talmud, however, does not end with God's laughter over God's own defeat. The continuation is nothing less than stunning:

> It was said: On that day all objects which R. Eliezar had declared clean were brought and burnt in the fire. They took a vote and excommunicated him. Said they, "Who shall go and inform him?"
>
> "I will go," answered R. Akiba, "lest an unsuitable person go and inform him, and thus destroy the whole world."
>
> What did R. Akiba do? He donned black garments and wrapped himself in black, and sat at a distance of four cubits from him.
>
> "Akiba," said R. Eliezar to him, "what has particularly happened today?"
>
> "Master," he replied, "it appears to me that thy companions hold aloof from thee." Thereupon he too rent his garments, put off his shoes, removed his seat and sat on the earth, whilst tears streamed from his eyes.
>
> The world was then smitten: a third of the olive crop, a third of the wheat, and a third of the barley crop. Some say, the dough in women's hands swelled up. A Tanna taught: Great was the calamity that befell that day, for everything at which R. Eliezar cast his eyes was burned up.

R. Gamaliel too was travelling in a ship, when a huge wave arose to drown him. "It appears to me," he reflected, "that this is on account of none other but R. Eliezer b. Hyrcanus."

Thereupon he arose and exclaimed, "Sovereign of the Universe! Thou knowest full well that I have not acted for my honor, nor for the honor of my paternal house, but for Thine, so that strife may not multiply in Israel!" At that the raging sea subsided.

Ima Shalom was R. Eliezer's wife, and sister to R. Gamaliel. From the time of this incident onwards she did not permit him to fall upon his face [to pray privately]. Now a certain day happened to be New Moon, but she mistook a full month for a defective one. Others say, a poor man came and stood at the door, and she took out some bread to him. [On her return] she found him fallen on his face [that is, at prayer]. "Arise," she cried out to him, "thou hast slain my brother."

In the meanwhile an announcement was made from the house of Rabban Gamaliel that he had died. "Whence dost thou know it?" he questioned her. "I have this tradition from my father's house: All gates are locked, excepting the gates of wounded feelings." (Baba Mezi'a 59b)

Following this astounding conclusion, the Gemara contains only a few more remarks, all of them related to wronging or shaming, but none of them directed to the story itself. Then the Gemara comes to an end, and the next portion of the Mishnah moves on to other matters.

INTERPRETATION BEYOND WORDS:
THE PRIVILEGE OF TEARS

It is hard to imagine a sharper turn than the one accomplished between the account of God's laughter and the events that immediately follow. But there had been a hint, if one had caught it. The citation "After the majority must one incline" is taken from Exod 23:2, as the commentary notes. The actual passage reads, "You shall not follow a multitude to do evil; nor shall you bear witness in a suit, turning aside after a multitude, so as to pervert justice." The interpretation of the verse given in the story is exactly the opposite of the verse's meaning in context. It requires, in fact, not just lifting out of context, but the re-writing of the text itself to give the verse R. Jeremiah's meaning.[6] There had been hint of what was to come.

"On that day," that is, the day of the report, everything Eliezar had declared clean was brought out and burned. What word is there for such a thing? The Sages had triumphed, over Eliezar and God both. Now the triumph unfolds with a smell of smoke. God had said that in all halachic matters the law was according to Eliezar. Perhaps that is why all things are burned. But what is the sense of the burning? What is really being burned? Testimony is being burned; the silent testimony of objects, objects that have become signs now. They all do testify, after all. Their existence keeps the question of the Sages' authority perpetually open. Eliezar can be silenced, but objects-become-signs cannot. They will speak beyond argument, and beyond the power of argument to defeat. They will declare. To silence them, they must be destroyed.

Next it is Eliezar who must be silenced. Akiba knows the danger of it. It is one thing to decide; it is another thing to put the decision into words. The wrong words will do the wrong thing; the wrong words will destroy the world. Akiba goes in mourning and sits at a distance. Let Eliezar see and ask, and then the words will be right. The question is asked. Akiba answers without answering. Eliezar is a man of signs. Let him read one sign more; let him read the clothing and the distance between himself and the others; let him be the one to say if something must be said. Eliezar answers with tears.

Akiba's strategy fails. There is something more powerful than arguments or signs or even prayer. There are tears, and tears will be heard when nothing else is. Eliezar asks no signs now; the stream of water is his own. There is no sound of laughter reported from Heaven. To the smoke of the ban is joined another smoke, for Eliezar's tears burn, and his look destroys. At sea, Gamaliel (Gamaliel II) the head of the House of Hillel, and head of the Council which excommunicated Eliezar, is nearly overcome by the waves which rise to drown him. Signs prove nothing, the Sages had said, but Gamaliel reads this sign clearly enough and calls to God. He protests that the ban is necessary for the peace of Israel. It is not a matter of power, he declares, but peace. What kind of peace and at what price he does not say. Peace from what? From Eliezar? From the clash of words and signs? Peace from an endless search beyond the texts for a more certain revelation? An end to wandering with no center? It is one thing to have a word-world that has no limits; it is very different to have one with no center. The sea subsides, yet the story continues.

Gamaliel's sister Ima Shalom, wife to Eliezar, understood. She kept watch to prevent her husband from praying his own prayers, afraid that his tears would come again. Even the Eighteen Benedictions may not be heard—the great prayer of the Rabbis—but tears will be heard. Then one day there is a lapse, and she returns to find that her fear has been realized. Eliezar has cried out once again. He has cried out at the wrong done to him, and those who cry out will be heard. She knows what must happen. Her brother will die for this deed done to Eliezar. The head of the House of Hillel, the one who presides in the place of authoritative speech, must pay the final price. The story finally comes to a close, a great tragedy, focused upon the words of one, perhaps the only one, who is entirely a victim and innocent: "All gates are locked excepting the gates of wounded feelings."

What has become of our happy story of God laughing? What has become of the triumph of interpretation? Who now is vindicated? Who was right? What does this mean all together? The questions grow and multiply. They re-open the "closed" story and jam it open. Too much is in opposition. The story cannot be resolved. It remains as a question, not an answer. What kind of story is this?

Overreaching, words, wrong, shame, the bloodless face, tears, the gates of the cries of the wronged, Heaven closed, prayer, law, an encompassing snake of words, all the arguments in the world, proof, sign, tree, stream, a Heavenly Voice, Scripture, God, laughter, defeat, burning, banning, mourning, streams of tears, calamity in the earth, the sea, petition, falling on the face, the death of the head of the interpretive house, the open gates of wounded feelings . . .

Eliezar is right. Joshua is right. Eliezar is wrong. Joshua is wrong. God is right. God is wrong. All of these are right. All are wrong. There is only one constant, one reading that is not undone, and remains as a judge of each interpretation, whether of this story or any other: there is wrong done by words, and the cries of those wounded by words will be heard in Heaven, and God will take their side.

THE EXEGESIS OF TEARS

We can never finish with stories such as these; we only lay them aside for a while to collect some threads of thought and see what they make. Reading and thinking about these ancient stories has indeed raised questions for me. They are not new questions, but they are important. These stories have led me back to them by a different route, to emerge on a different side of the clearing and to see, therefore, from a new perspective.

I find myself returning to the questions with which we began: questions of meaning, authority, community, interpretation, sacredness. Through the lens of this story I see that those questions must withstand a judgment, the judgment of tears. To take seriously the weight of the story I would have to come to the work of interpretation as an exegesis of tears, for tears are the human speech God privileges above all others. The story does not explain, but only declares that this is true. This is a truth to be learned, perhaps in a different way, from the Christian gospel as well.

An exegesis of tears would ask what meaning has to do with tears. An exegesis of tears would ask what our understanding of authority has to do with the tears around us, and what authority those tears have. It would ask about the community of tears; it would ask how tears interpret; it would ask about the sacredness of tears, the revelation of tears. Interpretation, understood through this story, would exist because of tears and for the sake of tears. Only with the wiping away of tears, only with the last of tears, would interpretation come to an end.

Through the lens of this passage of the Talmud, there is indeed a sign which is sovereign among the signs humankind makes: the sign of tears. There is also a speech which is privileged and takes precedence over other speech, even speech in the words of scripture: the cries of the wronged. The cries of the wronged both prove and declare. They can never be the interruption of interpretation, for they are its reason for being and its judge.

THE PROCESS OF INTERPRETATION AND THE SHAPE OF COMMUNITY

The story also has something to say about the relationship of interpretive authority and community. Interpretation is part of an "economy." That economy is both literal and figurative. We have learned that the literal economics of interpretation are a great enemy, and there are few who have not lost many battles against it. Interpretation is bought and sold, which means that it has a price. Who pays the price of interpretation? For whom is our interpretation most costly? Whose lives pay the price? Tears will tell us if we read them carefully.

There is a wrong done by interpretation like the wrong done by "overreaching." There is an overvaluing of certain interpretations and an undervaluing of others. The story teaches, as does the Mishnah, that there is a scale which weighs and gives true value. Can any interpretation be worth any value we choose to give it? No, the text teaches. Every interpretation must be weighed against tears, and tears will show its true value.

What makes a particular *reading* of a sacred text authoritative for a community? How does a community arrive at that reading? These are questions about the relationship between an authoritative text and its authoritative interpretation that an exegesis of tears raises. I am increasingly convinced that this is *the* question that enacts the essential shape of the community. Quite apart from any particular interpretation or body of interpretation, the *process itself* demonstrates what the community is. Interpretation, we might say, is a figure or an icon of community. The location of interpretive authority, therefore, patterns the shape of community. A community lives out a pattern of interpretive authority, and recreates that pattern at level after level of its own life.

It is an insight that comes from, among other sources, contemporary feminist theologians, that the community embodies—for good or for ill—interpretive authority. The fundamental shape, the social structure of a community, is its interpretive process writ large. That is, the shape of a community is a direct result of *who* has say in the interpretation of its central texts and its situation, who has *no say*, and how that is decided—*how* the conflict of interpretation is adjudicated, and what happens to the voices of those whose interpretations are not granted authority.[7]

To open the process of interpretation, therefore, beyond the guild of interpreters who have accepted (or taken) the authority to say what meaning is, is revolutionary. A process that is more open, plural, social, and dialogical, changes a community. Even if the products of interpretation remain essentially the same, the community will change. The broader the community of interpretation, the more complex and difficult it will be to define its identity. But its identity will also be more fully formed. It will be more fully formed because it will more nearly reflect the actual breadth of the community's life.

It is important to recognize, however, that community is also an enemy of interpretation, because community is essentially conservative. That does not mean conservative as opposed to radical, for certainly there are radical communities. Rather, it means conservative of its own identity and continuity, its own tradition of interpretation. Community *is* interpretation. It is a shared reading of a text, or a story, or an experience, or a world. The individual reading—the critical reading that cannot be assimilated into the central account—threatens the community's existence. The reading that changes the central account changes the community, and it is the nature of communities to resist such a change. What becomes of the "variant" readings that call a community's mythology and identity into question is a community's crucial test. How are they received? How are they preserved? What authority are they granted? How does the community understand the place of such readings?

THE EXPERIENCE OF SACREDNESS, THE EXPERIENCE OF MEANING

Finally, we come to the question of sacredness and meaning. Rather than ask *what* the sacredness of a text is, or *where* the sacredness is located, our story has turned our gaze in a different direction. It seems that the *what* and *where* of it have everything to do with the *when* of it. The sacredness of a text is something that happens, not something that is. Sacredness is the happening of meaning; not the meaning of the text, but the meaning that happens because of the presence of the text. It is not necessarily the meaning of the text, however, but the meaning that happens because of the presence of the text. That is, it is a question of ritual in which repetition takes precedence over interpretation. Sacredness *is* meaning in this sense. Meaning is not so much content—a *particular* meaning. Rather, the presence and repetition of the sacred text is what gives a time meaningfulness.

The adaptation that interpretation makes possible to the community lies less in the extension of a sacred text to show one how to walk in a new time, less in its wisdom, story, or parable, to tell one how to think, and more in the very ritual of interpretation. For interpreters of sacred texts, that may be midrash's chief gift to us. The ritual *is* the adaptation. The adaptation to the new time is the ritual itself.

Meaning is less a content, then, than an experience. Meaning is an experience, let us say, of connection, rootedness, "matteredness," reconciliation of life's deepest contradiction, participation in the mystery of truth and its unfolding. It would not be wrong to call such an experience sacred. People will search for such experience all their lives; and some, in the courage of such experience, will even lay their lives down.

There is an Hasidic tale from the Holocaust about the arrival of Hanukkah at Bergen-Belsen. As the time approached, the guards made a random selection of prisoners for beating and execution. The horror continued until sundown, the time for kindling the Hanukkah lights. From their tatters the prisoners constructed wicks and a hanukkhiah, and with the bodies of the dead lying outside the door, the Rabbi of Bluzhov lit the first light and began to chant the blessings. When he reached the third blessing, however, he stopped. He turned to the others as if searching for something, and then resumed the third blessing: "Blessed art Thou, O Lord our God, Ruler of the Universe, who has kept us alive, and has preserved us and enabled us to reach this season."

When the ceremony was over, one of those in attendance took the Rabbi aside and called him to account. How could one say such a blessing? With what had happened that very day, with the innocent suffering of the living and dead alike, and with no freedom in sight, how could one call this preservation and thank God? The Rabbi of Bluzhov responded,

> When I reached the third blessing, I also hesitated and asked myself, what should I do with this blessing? I turned my head in order to ask . . . the other distinguished rabbis who were standing near me, if indeed I might recite the blessing. But just as I was turning my head, I noticed that behind me a throng was standing, a large crowd of living Jews, their faces express-ing faith, devotion, and concentration as they were listening to the rite of the kindling of the Hanukkah lights. I said to myself, if God, blessed be He, has such a nation that at times like these . . . [when] death is looking from every corner, if despite all . . . they stand in throngs and with devotion listen-ing to the Hanukkah blessing . . . if, indeed, I was blessed to see such a people with so much faith and fervor, then I am under a special obligation to recite the third blessing. (in Yaffa Eliach 1982:14-16)

This is the authoritative interpretation of a sacred text.

4

THE
EXEGESIS
OF
ECHOES

LEANING OVER THE PAGE

When thinking about the situation of interpretation it is good to think about the preacher. In the person of the preacher certain human dimensions of the problem of interpretation become visible. In the preacher one encounters a *person* who must live in a self-conscious way on the margin, at a place where boundaries meet. There we can see how the different dimensions of interpretation arrange and rearrange themselves; how texts and time and community—history, place, relationships, death, worship, love, money, estrangement, secrets, lies, family, pain, work, expectation, suffering, justice, birth, prayer, and more—are real, unavoidable, and *properly* part of interpretation. In the preacher one can see with particular clarity an interpretation driven toward the experience of meaning, driven by the need for meaning in the life of a particular community.

The experience is familiar. The preacher sits before a portion of scripture, the text for the coming Sunday, having recognized long since that one's own small knowledge and experience and wisdom cannot meet the need of the community which will gather. The preacher leans over the text hoping the words will speak, so the preacher, too, will have something to say. The preacher leans over the text wanting to say what the lesson says: not merely to repeat an order of words, but to speak the text into life for a particular place and time, to speak the *fullness* of the text. To say what the text says, however, one must first *hear* what the text says; to hear what the text says, one must *read.*

Our problem has never been that the text has too *little* to say. It is rather that the text says so much, and evokes so much that it threatens to overwhelm us. There are echoes and harmonies, resonances and reverberations, relationships, patterns woven into the surface and color stained deep in the background. It is all filled with meaning, but what meaning? How do you begin to attend to it all? Faced with such extravagance of meaning the preacher may well grasp for the word closest to hand—a moral, a lesson, a piece of advice, or nothing more than an ancient illustration—and turn away to the simpler task of putting one's own thoughts in order. Surely it has happened to us all. Just as surely, though, we are all haunted by what we have left behind, by the voices of the text which whisper just at the edge of our hearing.

"Speak and bear witness," says Rilke. "*Read* and speak and bear witness," we might respond. The first and most difficult problem of interpretation is this problem of reading. Reading is where interpretation is born. It is in reading that the text's echoing voices are first summoned, silenced, honored or ignored. It is in reading that our most basic instruction in interpretation comes.

Yet this reading can be extraordinarily difficult. Eyes move automatically; one is scarcely more aware of reading than of breathing. The difficulty is all the greater when the text at hand is familiar. Then the reader has not only read, but has already interpreted. Certain voices have been privileged, certain choices made, and it is the text of those voices and choices which the reader meets; in the familiar text the voice which speaks most strongly is the reader's own. The preacher leans over the page to read. It is at once most basic and most difficult. Where can we find help in reading?

To explore one approach to reading we shall begin with two (perhaps unlikely) conversation partners: a story from the

Hebrew Bible and an essay by a poet/critic. These will then be combined with certain poststructuralist perspectives on the intensification of reading, called "reader-response" criticism. Finally, we will return to the situation of the preacher and the exegesis of echoes.

HEARING THE MELODY

The "Binding of Isaac" in the book of Genesis has had for many a deep magnetic pull. As a *reader* I have found myself drawn to it and wondering why. Why am I pulled here again and again? Although I know the story beginning to end, although I can tell the story and have, why do I return to *read* it? There would seem to be a special experience which the *reading* of the story itself provides. But what experience is it? What am I hearing? What am I overhearing?

Robert Creeley (1982:76) once observed that in a poem "I tend to hear whatever can be called its melody long before I have reached an understanding of all that it might mean." Words, it seems, may be haunted by more than sense. Melody and music are terms which have figured prominently in our appreciation of poetry, of course, but a narrative, too, may have a "melody" as well as a plot. The words which tell the story do more than simply convey who, what, when, where, why and how. They relate not only to the events they depict, but to each other. It is these relationships that we could call melody. Vocabulary, style, rhythm, sound, syntax, and other such factors are as much at work melodically in a narrative as in a poem. With Creeley we may well hear such a melody before we fully grasp the sense.

We could shift the musical analogy slightly and think of melody as plot. Are there harmonies being struck above and below the melody line of the story which we do not so much hear as overhear? Are there effects of language, of narration, of technique, which stamp a character upon the story? If there are, would they not shape our experience of the story as powerfully as harmony shapes our hearing of melody? The problem is how to approach and discover what lies so close to the threshold of hearing. How can I attend more fully both to the story at hand

and to my own responses? Are there approaches to reading which open up relationships, tensions, connections, that otherwise remain below the level of my awareness?

The second partner in this conversation is an essay by the poet and critic Denise Levertov, "On the Function of the Line" (1982:265-72). Her essay centers upon the ways line break and stanza shape the interpretation of a poem, emphasizing and de-emphasizing, muting and bringing forward, creating tensions and relationships which the prose line does not. Line and stanza, she argues, shape the unfolding experience and perception of a poem, so that the reader is presented not only with the completed expression but with the *process* of coming to expression. They are forms of punctuation which are a-logical, interpretive, supplementary; they embody instruction to the reader within the poem itself. As interpretive scoring, she maintains, they are especially important for the more "open" forms of poetry which must rely upon their own particular logic for achieving form, rather than utilizing a so-called "closed" poem form such as a triolet or a sonnet.

The argument of a modern poet, the tale of an ancient story-writer, and the question of a wondering reader may speak to one another. What if the "Binding of Isaac" were approached with the tools of line and stanza in hand? Could they help a reader open up the experience of reading? Could they help bring to awareness some of the echoes a reader overhears? Could they help an interpreter explore not only the plot and outcome of the story, but the effect and importance of how that story comes to expression?

TO READ A LINE

How do line and stanza function in non-metrical, "open forms" of poetry? Levertov argues that the open forms present a more exploratory experience of poetry. They are more concerned with revealing the way in which poetry happens, and not only the resulting poem.

> . . . such poetry, more than most poetry of the past, incorpo-
> rates and reveals the *process* of thinking/feeling, feel-

ing/thinking, rather than focusing more exclusively on its *results*; and in so doing it explores (or can explore) human experience in a way that is not wholly new but is (or can be) valuable in its subtle difference of approach: valuable both as human testimony and as aesthetic experience. And the crucial precision tool for creating this exploratory mode is the line-break. (1982:266)

Line break is a "parallel punctuation," as are the other variables of poetic form. The way lines are clustered or distanced from one another, the relative position on the page, the length and degree of closure a line achieves, endstopping, enjambment—these matters of form all function to interpret the reading of the poem, and they all relate to the line break.

As punctuation, the line break has, first of all, a rhythmic function: it creates a pause. The purpose of the pause is not found in logic or syntax, but in the process of writing itself. It records a moment of question and decision, as one asks, "who?" "what?" "how?" The pause is only momentary, however, a glimmer of hesitation, an eye which narrows slightly but does not blink. One possibility will be chosen and other possibilities will be rejected. The pause is the instant before the choice is made. There is no other punctuation which can record the hesitation. A dash is too abrupt, and a comma is too long. Call it a half-comma, perhaps, as others have. It creates what Levertov terms an "a-logical counter-rhythm," which combines with the "logical rhythm of syntax" to create "an effect closer to song than to statement, closer to dance than to walking" (1982:266).

The effect, however, is more than some counterpoint or syncopation of rhythm—and this is one of Levertov's principal points—because the pause "allows the reader to share more intimately the experience that is being articulated" (266). The reader is poised before the choice. We know the last word of the line and dwell upon it, however briefly, because this is the achieved point from which the choice must be made. We anticipate and propose, perhaps we expect, and then confront the actual word which begins the next line. The reader may be confirmed or puzzled or surprised—there are many possibilities—but in any case there is a tension and resolution which draws the reader further and further into the writing.

In standing before the unspoken "who?" or "what?" or "how?" the reader is drawn both backwards and forwards within the poem. There is, we could say, a crystallization of what the poem has been to that point. To choose or anticipate, the reader must risk an interpretation of what has gone before. That interpretation is not so much of a *propositional* kind, saying what the poem up to that point means. Rather, it is an interpretation of a *participational* kind. The reader, we could say, attempts to be conformed to the voice of the writing, to move into the writing itself. The anticipation goes beyond the choice of a word, of course. To propose even the single word requires an interpretation of what the poem will become from that point on. Both interpretations, backwards and forwards, are corrected by the poem itself. The perspective of the reader is thereby drawn increasingly into that of the writer. Perspective, however, is a visual term; better to say the voice of the reader is drawn increasingly into the voice of the writer.

The more important, and less understood, function of the line break for Levertov, has to do with its effect upon the melody of the poem. Rhythm is a monotone drum, melody rises and falls. The slight hesitation, the slight emphasis and de-emphasis, the weighing of a word's importance by its position in a line, all alter the pattern of pitch which the reader intones.

The line and stanza breaks create a kind of score which shapes the reading and speaking (or perhaps speaking first, then reading) of the words, in order to create a pattern for the whole. The reader of the poem, with the help of these formal "instructions," attempts to voice the parts so they may be heard in their most expressive relationship. Their placement in each instance gives a nuance which is difficult (if not impossible) to explain, but quite possible (if not easy) to pronounce. These nuances are as vital to the experience of the poem as the order of words and the sense they make.

Instructions for reading are foundational to interpretation, for interpretation is founded upon a reading. To voice the words of a text may be the most basic interpretive act. It is the first interpretation, which discloses a range of choices, and which subsequent interpretation expands or corrects; it is also a final interpretation, based upon all the interpretation which has occurred. We voice a reading in order to interpret, and that interpretation creates our subsequent reading. If every interpretation depends upon a pre-understanding or fore-understanding, voicing is a fundamental presentation of that understanding. The outer voice commits the reader to choices—to relationships, to nuances, to inflections—which the inner voice does not. The outer voice requires a precision of interpretation, and a pressing of interpretation in the presentation of the text itself.

Although Levertov's essay does not explicitly place itself in one or another critical stream, it has clear affinities with what is called "reader-response" criticism. By emphasizing the effect upon the reader, focusing on the process of reading and writing, and developing a reading-writing model which draws together the event-full and temporal character of reading, Levertov's work finds parallels in reader-response critical literature.[1]

In the relationship of reading and writing there is an understanding which is of special importance. "Reading and writing join hands, change places, and finally become distinguishable only as two names for the same activity" (Tompkins 1980:x).[2] Wolfgang Iser (1980:50-69), for example, has explored the question of reading process and interpretation in ways which speak to the project at hand. Iser's phenomenology of reading has strong similarities to the process Levertov describes, but explores the implications more deeply.

In Iser's model of reading, the reader becomes a co-creator of the work through the process of reading. Two phenomena in that process fit closely with Levertov. The first is the movement of what Iser calls retrospection and anticipation. We continually read backwards and forwards from what has been written to what shall be written. Sentences are previews of what will come and interpret what will come. What comes interprets what has gone before and brings it into some particular relationship, thereby suggesting still another range of possibilities for the future. "In whatever way, and under whatever circumstances the reader may link the different phases of the text together, it will always be the process of anticipation and retrospection that . . . transforms the text into an experience for the reader" (Iser 1980:56). The literary work is found, then, neither strictly in the text nor strictly in the reader, but squarely between the two.

The text which unfolds smoothly and obviously gives us nothing to do and we lose interest. There is neither opportunity nor need for our involvement. But where the smooth "flow" of a text is interrupted, where the retrospection and anticipation are suddenly experienced as inadequate to what occurs next in the text, the reader's participation is greatly heightened. Now we must take responsibility; now we enter into "writing." Thus breaks or "blockages" become essential to the reading process because they involve the reader in the process of co-creation.

A similar and related participation is what Iser calls the formation of "gestalts" of the literary text. By this he means the process of grouping together all the different aspects of a text to form a consistent pattern. While expectations may be continually modified, and images continually expanded, the reader will still strive, even if unconsciously, to fit everything together (58).

The reader is the one who groups the different parts of a text. The reader is the one who discerns a pattern and a direction and projects expectations. As new material threatens the gestalt, the material is either suppressed or the gestalt is revised. "In a process of trial and error, we organize and reorganize the various data offered us by the text . . . trying to fit them together in a way we think the author meant them to be fitted" (62). Thus the reader "recreates" the work through this dynamic process, a process which depends precisely upon interruption, the opening and reopening of the possibilities of a text.

Interpretation which attends to such a reading process looks through a powerful lens. The succession of words in time becomes the focus; each word, each cluster, line, phrase, sentence becomes the occasion for a renewed interpretive act. As Stanley Fish (in Tompkins 1980:xvi) writes, "Essentially what the method does is to *slow down* the reading experience so that 'events' one does not notice in normal time, but which do occur, are brought before our analytical attention." Criticism seeks to describe that experience. It is not only the critic, however, who is interested in the experience. The preacher leaning over the page, wanting to hear, needing to read, may also be interested.

We return to the question: What if the "Binding of Isaac" were approached with the tools of line and stanza in hand? Could they help a reader open up the experience of reading? Could they help an interpreter explore not only the result of the story, but the effect and importance of how that story comes to expression? Could they help hold the echoes?

THE BINDING OF ISAAC

We turn now to the story itself as one reader approaches it. The narrative will be presented in episodes. Each episode is judged to have achieved either a certain tension or resolution which makes it a useful literary unit for our purposes. After each section we will discuss selected aspects of the lines presented.

1

God tested Abraham
And said
To him,
          "Abraham!"

          "Here am I,"

He replied.

          "Take your son,
          Your only son
          Isaac
          Whom you love,

          And go to the land
          Of Moriah.

          Offer
          Him
          There

          As a burnt offering
          Upon one of the mountains
          Which I

          Shall tell you."

The particular choices aim to bring forward particular dynamics of the opening of the story. The language is supremely bare. Its tension and horror depend in large part upon the starkness of the saying: the call; the three- or four-fold naming of Isaac; the irony of Abraham being shown another land by God (as in the beginning of his story) but with a seemingly terrible purpose now; and the retardation of the command until its full weight may be seen balanced against God's original call, promise, guidance, and blessing, mirrored and recalled by the beginning of the dialogue. At the very outset, the story is thick with allusion and implication. It is densely patterned. It does not stand alone. It begins surrounded by echoes, echoes which sound precisely because of the bare clarity of the telling.[3]

One particular ordering holds open the tension. Rather than placing the imperative, "go to the land of Moriah" together with "upon one of the mountains which I shall tell you," the text is divided by the command to sacrifice: "offer him there." The effect is to maintain maximum attention upon the agency of God in the horrible deed. God's speech concludes not with Abraham or Isaac, but with the emphasis on God's saying.

The inauguration of the story profoundly shapes the relationship of the reader to what unfolds. The effect is a kind of immobilization and isolation of the reader. "God tested Abraham," the narrator says. The reader knows that what unfolds is a test, and that it is indeed God who sets everything in motion, but the characters in the story know nothing of the sort. Within the action itself, the speaker is unidentified except by the calling of Abraham's name. And Abraham's reply is at least as terse. No reciprocal naming, only the bare statement. The reader knows who speaks, but how does Abraham know? Could this as well be the voice of Satan as of God? As the incomprehensible command unfolds the question becomes more acute. How could this be? Who is God who could say this?

The reader knows it is a test. What does such knowledge do? The effect is not to soften the story but to make it more strange and distant. There is something unreal at hand. God speaks, but it is not really the word of God. God commands, but gives a false command. Everything which unfolds is founded upon a fiction; everything which unfolds is a kind of theater. Such a fiction puts the reader in a curiously paralyzed position. One cannot identify with Abraham because this crucial knowledge which determines everything is not shared. The reader knows, but Abraham does not, and the knowledge that this is a test throws a greater gulf between Abraham and the reader than culture or epoch ever could. One can neither rebel nor obey, because one cannot say what rebellion or disobedience are. We cannot take Abraham's role and rebel, for it is only a test: God has not truly commanded the sacrifice. We cannot obey and sacrifice Isaac, for it is only a test: God has not truly commanded the sacrifice. Or is that the very point of the test? Is the point of the test to obey by refusing? There is no hint. Yet of this fundamental tension, which so shapes the reader's perception of everything that is said and done, the human characters of the story are unaware. The reader's entry into the story cannot be through Abraham, for the story he lives and the one we read are two different stories. We cannot participate. We can only watch and listen, in a certain horror, as the story unfolds.

2

So Abraham
Rose early in the morning,
Saddled his ass,
Took two of his young men with him,

And his son,

Isaac;

And he cut
The wood
For the burnt
Offering,

And arose and went
To the place
Which God
Had told him.

On the third day
Abraham lifted up
His eyes

And saw

The place

Afar off.

In contrast to the beginning of the story, this segment is pure narration. The perspective is external to the characters. We see through no one's eyes but the narrator's, and the narrator's eyes are fixed upon Abraham. He is the subject of all the verbs.

Since the initial response to God Abraham has not spoken. What he thinks or feels cannot be read, and can scarcely be read *in*. The verbs are neutral and the actions closed. With so little to go on, the temptation is strong to project emotion into the small gap (or is it a gap?) which seems to appear with the comment that "Abraham lifted up his eyes." A three-day journey with lowered eyes? That must tell us something about this character so strongly walled off from us! But nothing is there. He lifts his eyes but they do not open onto him. We look for his eyes but can only follow where they gaze: the place, afar off.

In this portion, too, the reader's immobility and externality are reinforced. We see the picture but cannot hear the sound which might interpret for us, or bring us *inside*. No one speaks to include us. Having spoken, God is silent; having heard, Abraham is silent; witnessing, the reader is silent.

The retardation of the naming of Isaac appears here, as in the initial sequence. The effect is double. On the one hand it expresses reluctance and pathos, building the sense of both the unthinkable and the inevitable. Must Abraham? Will Abraham? On the other hand it expresses a distancing of Abraham from Isaac, which stands in grim contrast to the relational insistence of the narrator that this is "his son, Isaac." This wrenching irony will grow and deepen frighteningly in the events to come. Abraham is subject, Isaac is object; Abraham takes, Isaac is taken; between father and son all those verbs, those acts, those intentions, intervene.

An ironic foreshadowing has begun, and with it a pattern of double irony which marks the story as a whole. Abraham *cuts* the wood; later he will take the knife to cut his son. He cuts the wood for the offering. It is, indeed, the wood for the burnt offering, but not the one Abraham has been commanded to make. The end is present in the middle, both the anticipated end and the unanticipated one. Abraham *lifts up* his eyes to see the terrible hill, as he will again lift up his eyes from Isaac upon the altar to look upon the miraculous ram. These ironies only prepare for ironies much more strong and cruel, and perhaps even comic.

The positioning at the close of this portion reconfirms both the multiple distancing in the story and its effect of tension. As we are distanced from the characters, as Abraham is distanced from God, as father is distanced from son (and as the apparent future is distanced from the blessing of the past), so also is Abraham at this moment of crisis distanced from the place which God had indicated. He is *here*, and the place of God's command is *there*. Obedience is the distance between.

3

Abraham said
To his young men,

> "Stay here with the ass;
> I and the lad
> Will go
>
> Yonder
>
> And worship,
>
> And come again to you."

Abraham took the wood
    of the burnt offering
And laid it upon Isaac,
His son;

He took in his hand
The fire
And the knife.

So they went
Both of them
Together.

At last Abraham speaks; from Isaac there is still no word. The dramatic ironies are vivid on the page. They will indeed come again, although to Abraham that can only be a lie (in the end, it is true, only Abraham is named as returning, although Isaac lives; the force of that seems unclear). The wood is laid upon Isaac as Isaac will soon be laid upon the wood. The father takes in hand the fire and knife, not the son. Now they go together. Before, Isaac was the object to be taken by his father. Here they are subjects together. The victim trusts his executioner; the sacrifice carries his own pyre; the son obeys the father as the father obeys God. The dramatic ironies are vivid enough upon the page.

But is Abraham also being ironic when he says that he and Isaac will go and "worship and come again?" Why "worship" instead of "sacrifice"? The word choice seems so cruel. To obey is one thing. To obey through clenched teeth is one thing. To sacrifice your son is one thing. But to worship, that is another thing. The word becomes horrible in a way "sacrifice" does not. Worship itself takes on a possible danger and obscenity which calls worship itself into question.

If he is being ironic then at last we learn something of Abraham; we learn of rebellion, perhaps, or anger or resentment, but something, at least, through his own speech. If he is not being ironic, the mask remains. Who is being ironic, the narrator or Abraham? The story gives no further clues.

4

Isaac said to his
Father Abraham,

      "My Father!"

        "Here am I
        My son."

      "Behold the fire
      And the wood;
      But where is
      The lamb

      For the burnt offering?"

"God will supply
[God]self with the lamb
For a burnt offering,

My son."

So they went
Both of them
Together.

Son and father address one another. The pathos could scarcely be greater: the lamb asks about a lamb, and the father lies but tells the truth.

The Rabbis noted the famous ambiguity of "a burnt offering, my son," and the several ironies which may be elicited depending upon the punctuation.[4] The ironies reach back to the beginning and forward to the end. They reach even beyond the beginning to the miraculous conception of Isaac at the hand of God. The possible meanings do not so much invite the reader to unravel all the strands, but rather to see the possible meanings as an intricate constellation of ironies, viewed simultaneously.

Now Isaac is as incomprehensible as Abraham. Rabbinic commentaries introduce imaginary dialogues and internal monologues precisely as the story reaches its climax for this very reason. How could he? Why does he? Why doesn't he? But we can plumb no more of Isaac's character than we can of Abraham's. His words hide rather than reveal. This story is in some way without seams or gaps, and yet it gapes. It remains incomprehensible at its core, and there is no way in. And now, with the repetition of the solemn and ominous "So they went both of them together," yet another point of return is left behind. The only way out is the way through.

5

When they came to the place
Of which God
Had told him,
Abraham there built
An altar,

Laid
The wood in order
    and

Bound
Isaac
His son
    and

Laid him
On the altar
Upon the wood.

Then Abraham
Put forth
His hand
And took
The knife
To slay
His son.

Pure narration again, with pure pitiless verbs. The action unfolds in a kind of slow dream suddenly focused upon Abraham's hand. The building of the altar, the laying of the wood, the binding of Isaac and placing him upon the altar—each of these steps to the critical moment are indicated by their single and uncompromising verbs. But then the narrative turns to the deadly detail: the hand of Abraham stretches forth to take the knife. The effect in English is chilling as the tumble of stresses resolves into the sound of a heartbeat. The climax approaches on marching iambic feet.

6

But

An angel of the LORD
Called to him from heaven,
    and said

            "Abraham, Abraham!"

      "Here am I."

          "Do not lay your
          Hand on the lad,
          Or do

Anything
To him.

For now I know

That you fear
God,
Seeing you did not
    withhold

Your son,
Your only son,

From me.''

And Abraham lifted up
His eyes and looked,

And behold,

Behind him was
A ram
Caught in a thicket
By his horns;

Abraham went and took the ram
And offered it up

As a burnt offering

Instead
Of his son.

So Abraham called the name of that place,
The LORD will provide,

As it is said to this day,
"On the mount of the LORD,
It shall be,

Provided.''

Of Abraham we still know nothing; of Isaac we still know
nothing. The angel says what the angel knows, but the angel
apparently had only one question. The reader has many. The
end of the story for God is not the end for Abraham or Isaac or
the reader. Where the story ends, the questions begin.

In this climactic moment of the story the narrator seems to
turn for a moment to acknowledge the reader or hearer in direct

address. It is a small turn, accomplished in a single word: "Behold."

The isolation and immobilization of the reader, first established in the paralyzing beginning of the story, are confirmed. We have indeed been outside looking in; we have not been positioned to participate but to witness. We have not been positioned where we may understand but where we may see. The story does not give its meaning, but itself.

Look, says the narrator. Look at the moment opening up now, but remember it is a *story*, after all, told by a story-teller. You have been brought all this way to see this. The story has been told for you. Behold.

As Abraham turns to sacrifice the ram a gauze veil descends upon the events. They begin to retreat into the distance: Abraham, Isaac, the angel, the pyre, the ram, the knife, the fire, the hand. "As it is said to this day" (the narrator has turned fully now), "On the mount of the LORD it shall be . . . [What shall be? What will happen upon the mount of the LORD? This? Again?] . . . it shall be provided."

Have we been brought so far for this? For the narrator to turn to us with this word? Perhaps so. The word which *ends* the story, does not *still* the story. It only lets the reader and speaker rest—for a while. Neither the teller nor the hearer would pretend that the matter is settled. The closure is a fiction. But for now it will do, until the time comes to tell the story again. The story ends, but for the reader the rings begin to spread in every direction. Farther and farther they reach—spreading through the Bible, spreading through ourselves and what we know of the world, spreading through what we think and know (and think we know) of God. The rings grow larger and larger until they cannot be seen all at once, but only in small sections of an arc. Consider this question, formulate that problem, ponder one implication, probe another explanation—small sections of quickly retreating rings—until the distances grow too great, the connections too faint. Only in the story itself does it all hold. The story holds together what we cannot. When the threads break we turn, therefore, and once again begin to read.

HEARING ECHOES

Whatever echoes there are reverberating within the smaller world of the story and the larger world of the Story in which it is set, there are of course more echoes still. "Fraught with background," was the way Eric Auerbach described it (1965: 12). And the interpretation of the story is fraught with background as well. Many have gone before: great expositors of the scriptures, poets, critics, religious teachers, parents, and pastors. The story is so troubling that it may seem to require immediate interpretation, a way of limiting the possibilities—stilling the echoes—and saying what the story refuses to say: what it means. Perhaps many of us have even had one substituted for the other, and been given (or given) an explanation in place of a story. One must decide for oneself whether any of the explanations have been satisfying. But no interpretation has succeeded in quieting the questions the story provokes. Nevertheless, it is good to recall some of the approaches interpretation has taken.

In Hebrews we read this interpretation:

> By faith Abraham, when put to the test offered up Isaac. He who had received the promises was ready to offer up his only son, of whom he had been told, "It is through Isaac that descendants shall be named for you." He considered the fact that God is able even to raise someone from the dead—and figuratively speaking, he did receive him back. (Hebrews 11:17ff)

It was a matter of faith in the power of God, then, faith in the power to give life back from death. Abraham is one who considers power but not reasons. He considers what God can do, but not what God does, for faith is "the assurance of things hoped for, the conviction of things not seen. Indeed, by faith our ancestors received approval" (Hebrews 11:1-2). The story has meaning, therefore, as a part of the history of faith, including Abel, Enoch, Noah, Isaac, Jacob, Moses' parents, Moses himself, the people of Israel, and Rahab the prostitute. The names go on and on to include heroes, rulers, prophets, soldiers, judges, martyrs, refugees, and wanderers. All of them, however, in all their faith, in all their loss and gain, are seen as incomplete. The story of their faith requires completion, the author insists, in the faith of the present Christian community running the race set before them (Hebrews 11:40-12:2). The story of Abraham and Isaac is therefore one among many, and resolves into its essential, an essential shared with too many stories to tell (Hebrews 11:32). It is a story of faith. And it is told in order to join the story of the present community to the story of the past, and thereby to encourage the people to hold fast to faith themselves.

A different sort of faith is what certain rabbinic midrashim depict.[5] When God ordered Abraham to sacrifice Isaac, one story goes, Abraham held his tongue and did not point out how God's order contradicted God's promises. Instead, he kept his grief and his rebuke to himself until the angel came to turn him aside. But Abraham demanded something in return in order to turn aside from the sacrifice, Abraham demanded something in return. And so he extracted a promise that because of what he had done, because he had kept silent, so also in the future when his descendants broke God's law, God also would keep silent and forgive. "So be it," God agreed. "Let them but retell this tale and they will be forgiven."

Call it a story of encouragement, then, but of a different kind. Instead of an example of faith for the community to follow, the story becomes a claim for mercy. The story is told to remind God of God's promises, and to remind the people of how and why God has promised to forgive. Forgiveness rests upon the people because God and Abraham spoke together and acknowledged the claim each had upon the other. If Abraham can forgive God, how can God not forgive Israel?

Augustine (*City of God*, xvi.32) reads and finds a story of obedience. Abraham faces a temptation to disobedience, a temptation by which he was to attain to knowledge of himself, of his own faith. A divine command thunders. Abraham refuses dispute. He obeys. Why? Because he knows that God has promised to make of him, through Isaac, a great nation. Therefore, if God should order him to slay Isaac, then God would also restore Isaac to life. There is no contradiction. The promise of God endures, even when the command is incomprehensible. The promise comforts, even when the command torments. For even God in Christ endures the same contradiction for the deliverance of God's people (Romans 8:32). Augustine reads Abraham through the cross, and reads the cross through Paul. He sees, therefore, in the obedience of Abraham, the figure of God's own sacrifice, and in the renewed blessing of Abraham, he sees the figure of the redemption which flows from the cross.

Vault over some thirteen centuries and you find Luther lecturing on the story. He lectures amidst a plague, having buried a friend and colleague on the day before, and speaks to those who themselves are afraid for their own lives (*Lectures on Genesis*, 91 n.1). Luther speaks of the greatness and the singularity of Abraham's trial, in which he endures what no other patriarch could or would have to.

> But it is impossible to understand the greatness of his trial . . . This trial cannot be overcome and is far too great to be understood by us. For there is a contradiction with which God contradicts Himself. It is impossible for the flesh to understand this . . . I am unable to resolve this contradiction. Our only consolation is that in affliction we take refuge in the promise; for it alone is our rod and staff . . . These events are recorded for our comfort, in order that we may learn to rely on the promises we have. I was baptized. (93-94)

The great contradiction of which Luther speaks takes on deeply personal tones. One must conclude either that God is lying (a blasphemy) or that God hates me (which leads to despair). These are two unacceptable possibilities. The story, he insists, "cannot be explained in a manner commensurate with the importance of the subject matter" (93).

A striking remark. The story provokes what explanation cannot quiet. The story leads into the experience of despair, in particular the temptation to think that God does not want me to be saved, that the promises of baptism are somehow not for me. To read this story of Abraham is to be turned toward one's own deepest fear (in Luther's estimation, at least). It is more than a logical puzzle to be solved or a dilemma with which one simply lives. It is the experience of an utter contradiction at the very heart of one's life, the experience of a great division which cannot be negotiated and cannot be reconciled. From this contradiction one can only be saved.

The story cannot be understood. It can, however, lead anew to the source of comfort, the source for Abraham and the source for the faithful: the promise of God. The promise of God is greater than death, contradiction, reason, Satan, sin, suffering, doubt. The promise of God is greater than everything one sees, or fears, or imagines. It is the promise of resurrection, which overcomes everything, and upon which one may depend utterly both in life and in death. The story drives one to the limits of reason and the edge of the great abyss, which is also where the pure healing grace of promise is seen for what it is: the Word of God which endures forever.

Kierkegaard also found it necessary to speak of Abraham. In his own estimation, the long meditation of *Fear and Trembling* was (at least aesthetically) his finest work, enough alone to immortalize his name. It was also a reproduction, he confessed, of his own life to the time of its writing (1954:18). Through Abraham, Kierkegaard unfolded some of his most distinctive themes. He wrote of the paradoxical "teleological suspension of the ethical," in which the individual steps beyond the claims of universal laws and principles. He wrote of the absolute and singular, utterly unmediated quality of the relationship of an individual to God. He wrote of the movement of infinite resignation, the preparation of the paradox of faith in which one receives back again what has been surrendered.

Most of all, however, his meditation was upon the mystery and paradox of faith itself, which he called the highest passion of all (1954:131). And to gaze upon the mystery of faith, Kierkegaard gazed upon the face of the Abraham he imagined for himself. He dwelt upon the *human* mystery of Abraham. Whatever faith is, he insisted, it is only to be grasped in a finite person. Faith is not known in objectivity and from a distance, but, as he writes in his *Concluding Unscientific Postscript*, in the greatest intensification of subjectivity, that is, in passion (1941: 118).

Here is . . . a definition of truth: An objective uncertainty held fast in an appropriation-process of the passionate inwardness is the truth, the highest truth attainable for an existing individual . . . The truth is precisely the venture which chooses an objective uncertainty with the passion of the infinite . . . But the above definition of truth is an equivalent expression for faith. (1941:182)

The human mystery of Abraham, however, is never described in the story in Genesis. Only Abraham is there, in his words and deeds. The mystery which so deeply moved Kierkegaard was the mystery he met when he held Abraham up as a mirror to see himself. But this mirror was, in Kierkegaard's view, more than just a mirror upon himself. It was a door which led into the essentially human in its great contradictions of possibility and necessity, inwardness and outwardness, both the most extraordinary and most ordinary dimensions of human existence. "Faith has in fact two tasks," he wrote, "to take care in every moment to discover the improbable, the paradox; and then to hold it fast with the passion of inwardness" (1941:207).

Thus in Kierkegaard the echoes of earlier interpreters may be heard: questions of faith, questions of obedience, questions of personal despair. But in his hands the story becomes not a lesson, or an example, or a discourse on the nature of God, but a lead to sound the depths of the human soul.

Kierkegaard considered the story as a poet from Copenhagen; Wilfred Owen considered it from the trenches of the Western front in World War I. Owen was a British officer who wrestled poetry from the desperation and boredom of the soldier's life in war. It was not a popular poetry. His was not the sort of verse to inspire patriotic sacrifice, a quest for glory, and hatred of the enemy. For in his poems it was not the Germans who were the enemy; it was war and death, the enemy of all. Owen looked at the soldiers and saw Christ crucified.

Owen also saw, however, that there were human agents in this unholy pageant. In 1918 he wrote a poem titled "The Parable of the Old Man and the Young" (150).

So Abram rose, and clave the wood, and went,
And took the fire with him, and a knife.

And as they sojourned both of them together,
Isaac the first-born spake and said, My Father,
Behold the preparations, fire and iron,
But where the lamb, for this burnt-offering?
Then Abram bound the youth with belts and straps,
And builded parapets and trenches there,
And stretched forth the knife to slay his son.
When lo! an Angel called him out of heaven,
Saying, Lay not thy hand upon the lad,
Neither do anything to him, thy son.
Behold! Caught in a thicket by its horns,
A Ram. Offer the Ram of Pride instead.

But the old man would not so, but slew his son,
And half the seed of Europe, one by one.

In Owen's hands the horror of Abraham's sacrifice is turned back upon the world he knows. It is not ancient Abraham who is incomprehensible. He at least turned aside. However unfathomable the human drama of "The Binding of Isaac," with its strange collision of faith, love, command, testing, obedience, and horror, it is not a story of death, for Abraham turned aside. The poet saw reenacted in front of him the sacrifice which was not consummated that day. Each day, each death, one by one by one by one, in awful clarity, Owen saw the soldiers lifted onto the altar in sacrifice. A parable he called it, of the old man and the young. Whatever the strangeness and mystery of Abraham, he found the sacrificial slaughter around him to be more strange yet. It is as if to say, "Look to the mystery and horror on Mount Moriah, but ask no questions of the figures there; ask your questions of the old men who can see no other answer to their dilemma than the execution of their young. One by one." Wilfred Owen himself was killed on November 4, 1918, one week before the armistice.

Consider also the angle of vision of a contemporary poem by Bobbie Groth, "Isaac's Body."[6] In her poem also the scene is transformed. The three-day journey becomes an attempt to hide a terrible deed from the eyes of Isaac's mother. The altar of Moriah is transformed into a hospital bed upon which a young boy lies, a victim and survivor of his father's brutal incest. The talk of commitment, covenants, and God, are the lies and rationalizations of perpetual lust satisfying itself, excusing itself, and hiding the evidence of crime so the sacrifice may continue. The voice of Isaac's mother speaks:

> But you forget that I
>   really talk to God
> and it has nothing to do
>   with taking life
>   to show love
> It has to do
>   with snatching boy's bodies
>   off of hilltops
>   and bringing them
> to hospital rooms
>   to get better
> So they can hate me
>   and I can love them back
> and fight to undo
>   your despicable covenants

It never was the voice of God at all, the poem concludes. It was Satan's voice, the voice of Abraham's own lust, and he was too stupid to know the difference.

Like Wilfred Owen in his time, Bobbie Groth in hers looks into "The Binding of Isaac" and sees the very place in which she stands. Having seen that however, she turns back upon the original story to *charge* it with responsibility. The story is not really mysterious. What is mysterious is the inability to see through it and its kind, to see the horror it visits upon generation after generation—a horror perpetuated by interpretation focused upon "commitments, covenants, and God." The story is interpreted in order to shear it of its false and deceitful mystification, to say the unspeakable in the present, and to *be free* from the story at last.

Let us also take, as a final example, a recent commentary by Walter Brueggemann (1982). This work is located quite intentionally in the context of the preacher preaching within the Christian community. Recalling Luther, Brueggemann turns to the pastoral problem, the aspects of the community's experience to which the story may speak. He offers not so much an "explanation" of the story, but rather through the story he evokes and names dimensions of experience which are otherwise named neither so well, nor together. In doing so, however, Brueggemann does not focus upon human experience as such, but specifically upon a life lived within the language and story of Christian faith.

> The life of Abraham, then, is set by this text in the midst of the contradiction between the *testing* of God and the *providing* of God; between the sovereign freedom which requires complete obedience and the gracious faithfulness which gives good gifts; between the command and the promise; and between the word of death which takes away and the word of life which gives. (1982:192)

It is a story which speaks of faith, a faith not so much in the resurrection as a specific solution to a specific problem (as with Luther), but in the more fundamental power of God as the power of resurrection working "against every deathly circumstance" (193). It is in Jesus that the dialectic of testing and providing reaches its supreme expression, and is transformed for the church into the dialectic of crucifixion and resurrection. The final word to the community, while it may be about faith, is not about the faithfulness of Abraham. It is about the faithfulness of God, the one who provides.

To interpret the story in this way, then, means to work within a particular language, a particular shared vocabulary of stories, laws, images, metaphors—a "canon" or "world," one might say—and through this tapestry of language to illuminate both the tapestry as a whole, and the particular part of it called "The Binding of Isaac." To do that is to illuminate, as well, the contemporary life which is lived within this same world.

Six interpretations spanning nineteen centuries. What do they share? They all share an attempt to interpret the story through an interpretation of a character, usually Abraham, sometimes God. They all attempt to discover, through an understanding of a *character*, the meaningfulness of the *narrative*. The events of the story, in all these interpretations, become intelligible (if at all) through the grasping of interior processes, motivations, feelings, and intentions. That is, the story becomes intelligible through supplying (to some degree) what is not given in the story, supplying the absence which makes the story so haunting.

Neither God nor Abraham in this story are given for our understanding, however. But if they are not given to be understood, then how are they given? To be remembered. They are given in such a way as to remain in the memory as themselves, not dissolved into qualities or examples or illustrations, but as two characters who can be neither forgotten nor understood, met together in a story which can be neither forgotten nor understood. The community must remember, like Abraham it must deal with this God, who is sometimes incomprehensible and horrifying, and in response to whom we too may become incomprehensible and horrifying, even and especially to ourselves.

Every story of God is haunted by the echoes of this story. Perhaps that is why Augustine and Luther and others felt it so necessary to "bind" it to the heart-most story of the Christian faith, the crucifixion and resurrection of Jesus. The embrace of any lesser story is too weak, and the strength of Mt. Moriah too great, simply to *hold* it. Such a story becomes bearable not through understanding, but only through the memory of another story which is stronger still.

To tell a story about God is to take up a grave responsibility. Just as the rabbi who bade his family a final farewell every morning before he prayed and called upon the Name (knowing how dangerous such a thing was), to tell a story about God is a grave matter. Because it is a story about God . . . Because it is a *story* about God . . . One story is never true enough. Tell one, and another must be told, and another, and another. Each one is a kind of blasphemy which can only be undone, repented, by another story, by telling what the one before did not, going farther and farther. Each story of God, therefore, is a kind of failure and a kind of sin; and each story a kind of praise, and confession, and amends. I tell a story of God because I have told stories. And now, therefore, I must tell another. It is the humility of God to be told into story. It is the glory of God to be told past *every* story forever. It is the glory of the community to tell; it is the humility of the community to begin again and again.

Under the sign of "The Binding of Isaac," interpretation is the exegesis of echoes. It is not about grasping a story's meaning, but a discovering and following of its echoes. Interpretation becomes a listening for the invisible but audible presence, the presence summoned and responding, set in motion, ringing as bells do when one of them is struck. It listens to the pressure upon the ear of memory, the overtones multiplying above other stories because the struck bell of this story so reverberates into the mystery and contradiction of a life. Interpretation marks how the story echoes into what is most dismaying and most comforting, what is most deeply feared and most deeply trusted. It follows the sight line of the eye which is opened by the story, the eye taught by the ear to see what was not seen before, the vision some call faith which trusts the ear more than the eye, reading neither light nor dark but only the Word. An exegesis of echoes *interprets* by bringing the echoes forward, giving a voice to what waits at the edge of speaking and hearing—telling into story what the echoes awaken, telling toward the stories of God, which once begun, tell forever.

5

THE
EXEGESIS
OF THE
UNWRITTEN

STORIES IN A DIFFERENT INK

How many ways stories are set down. How wonderful and fearful are the inks and the material of the page. How remarkable the elements that make the language. How charmed the reading may have to be, or how palpable the grasp of interpretation. Ink, blood, milk, water, wine, the food upon the table, the cloth upon the table, the cloth upon the body, the body touching the body, the language of hands and feet, tools, stars turning, days and nights.

There are so many who cannot *write* the story. There are so many who may not. There are so many who do not. Cannot because even the inscribing of a name is a mystery, because there is no time, because there is no luxury. May not because it is forbidden, because it is dangerous, because it just isn't done. Do not because there is a different language, because no one has asked, because the story has too much power.

The story, nevertheless, is told. Day calls to day, night unto night declares knowledge; there is no speaking or words, but still the voice goes as far as the farthest rim. The *Story* is always beginning, always unfolding, always ending, and always presenting itself to be read. Who can teach one to see and hear stories which are not written in words? Who can teach the passion of interpreting these? Who can teach the mystery of understanding these?

It is only a small irony that a person would *read* to learn interpretation of what has not been written. The fixity, the tangibility, the dissemination, the persistence and endurance of writing go far in making visible those who were always there, and making audible their stories. Through reading one discovers "texts" beyond the usual writing. One discovers texts inscribed in different ink, upon a different page, in a different "language," and according to different rules. Through reading one learns to look away from reading. One may also discover a different way of interpretation—where to stand, how to begin, how to look, how to hear, how to ask, how to refrain from asking, how to depart, how to keep silence, how to repeat.

This is true in the writing of certain women now. It is especially true of the writing that remembers those who cannot, may not, and do not write, and that remembers the reasons why. It is true of the writing that attempts to remember and retain in itself the different inks, pages, and languages to which the sisters and foremothers have turned. It is true of the writing that seeks to bring out from the shadows a bright cloth patterned by an art and intellect which sewed their threads according to a more open understanding of beauty and intelligence. It is true of writing in which the story of women telling the story is told.

The Danish author Karen Blixen, who wrote in the penname Isak Dinesen, was such a writer. Although she is probably known best now for the work *Out of Africa*, a quasi-autobiographical narrative of her life in Kenya, she also wrote deeply imagined, frequently interlocking, almost mythical tales. She wrote stories of women and men telling stories, hearing stories, hiding stories, taking and mistaking, creating and falsifying, believing and disbelieving, living by and for stories, and dying for them. Hers were tales about tales and their interpretation, stories which pressed toward the very questions of writing and reading confronting us here. Once viewed as a "popular" writer (which she certainly was in her own lifetime—a "merely" popular writer to many), more recent readings of her work have found perspectives, issues, and resources related to some of the most creative thinking—especially feminist thinking—in Europe and North America. Not the least of these issues are the questions of what a story is, how it is "written" and by whom, and what it means to read and interpret.

Here we shall consider two stories which unfold their questions in ways that are both particularly vivid and representative: "The Blank Page," and "The Caryatids." As elsewhere, the concern is with the stories themselves, the "worlds" they display, and how we might construe the work of interpretation under the signs of those worlds.

THE BLANK PAGE

"The Blank Page" belongs to *Last Tales* (1957). It is the conclusion of an unfinished set of stories originally intended to be a long collection of interlocking narratives called *Albondocani* (1957:99-105). The outline of the story can be sketched in fairly quickly, including some particulars of language to which we shall return.

By the gates of an unnamed ancient city sat an old veiled woman who made her living telling stories. Calling out to a lady and gentleman passing by, she offered to tell them a story and, by way of introduction, began to recite her own lineage. She was the granddaughter of a story-teller, a woman who had learned the art from her own grandmother. For five generations the women had been story tellers—some two hundred years—so long that they had become indistinguishable to the people of the city. They merged into one woman, perpetually old, who had told stories for two centuries. Her grandmother had taught her,

> "Be eternally and unswervingly loyal to the story . . . [for w]here the story-teller is loyal, eternally and unswervingly loyal to the story, there, in the end, the silence will speak. Where the story has been betrayed, silence is but emptiness. But we, the faithful, when we have spoken our last word, will hear the voice of silence.
>
> "Who then," she continues, "tells a finer tale than any of us? Silence does. And where does one read a deeper tale than upon the most perfectly printed page of the most precious

book? Upon the blank page . . . We," she says at last, "the old women who tell stories, we know the story of the blank page."

The old woman then began her tale of a Carmelite convent in the mountains of Portugal. The sisters there grew the finest flax with seed brought back from the Holy Land by a crusader, for as the story-teller says, "the very first germ of a story will come from some mystical place outside the story itself." From this flax they made beautiful linen which served as the bridal sheets for all the young princesses of the royal house.

After the wedding night the sheet would be solemnly displayed as testimony to the princess's virginity. The central part of the sheet was then cut out, framed, and returned to the convent, where it was hung in a great gallery with all the others, each marked with the name of the princess. To this gallery the women would return for many years as on a pilgrimage which was "by nature sacred and secretly gay."

There was also one highborn old woman who had never married who came. In her youth she had been a friend to one of the princesses, and she too would return to the gallery to gaze upon the canvases. In the figures and patterns she read omens and stories, predictions and events, comparing the fulfillment to the sign, "sighing a little and smiling a little. Each separate canvas with its coroneted name-plate has a story to tell, and each has been set up in loyalty to the story."

Among all these canvases, however, there was one which was different. For, "on this one plate no name is inscribed, and the linen within the frame is snow-white from corner to corner, a blank page. . . . [W]ith what eternal and unswerving loyalty has not this canvas been inserted in the row! The story-tellers themselves before it draw their veils over their faces and are dumb."

The women of the royal family and all their friends dwell there the longest, and there it is that the "old and young nuns, with the Mother Abbess herself, sink into deepest thought." This is the story of the blank page.

Let us begin with this triangle of story, story-teller, and silence. The old woman is insistent: there is more than just the teller and the tale; there is a third term which follows after them, a term which makes all the difference. There is what she calls "the silence." But strangely, the silence has a kind of voice, makes a kind of revelation. It reveals a relationship, the relationship of the teller to the story. The silence reveals loyalty or disloyalty. It reveals to the teller herself how things stand between her and what she has said. Is the silence emptiness or a voice? It cannot be said in advance. Either way, however, it is a sign, and it testifies, as all signs do, beyond the rules of argument.

The silence itself, then, becomes a story in turn. It becomes a story about a story and the one who told it, revealing loyalty or disloyalty. How can a story-teller be loyal or disloyal? Is it a matter of belief? Of memory? Of repetition? Of intention? Can I tell a story I believe in a way which makes it disbelief? Can I tell a story I do not believe in a way which makes it belief? Can I tell a lie that tells the truth and tell a truth that lies?

My own grandmother was a story-teller. Bible stories were her text, and she would tell them during long evenings playing canasta in her sitting room. A story was never the same twice. It was about the same character, perhaps, and the same events, but it was never repeated as if it had been memorized. The story was the same, but the words would be different. But how can that be? There are certainly different ways of *explaining* it. A structuralist could explain easily enough according to the particular functions of plot and character, or general linguistic competence. A student of oral "literature" could explain it according to the conventions of oral poetry, and its recitation and improvisation. I prefer the explanation of another story-teller I once asked. I told him about my grandmother, how she remembered but never memorized, and asked him what the difference was. He responded, "First of all, let me say your grandmother was a very wise woman. When you memorize a story you tell it because you can repeat the words. When you remember a story you tell it because you are there, where the story is."

Maybe this is what it means to be loyal. Maybe it means to remember, to live and speak—at least as long as the story lasts—in the world of that story. The story is not a narrative one speaks about, but a world in which one hears and sees, and from which one tells. Disloyalty would be the refusal to hear and see, the refusal to stand within. In disloyalty I would take my place *apart* from the story. This is not a question of being friend or enemy to the story, advocate or accuser, but a question of presence. Is the teller present in the telling? Only in being present to the story in the telling is the teller present to the hearer in the hearing. To be loyal is to be there. This is the loyalty of imagination.

If there is loyalty, the old woman promises, the silence will begin to tell a story, a deeper story than anyone could tell or write. What could such a story be? If this is a riddle then there is an answer. We try keys until one fits. Some sayings, however, are not meant to be answered; they mean to bring the enquirer to a crisis, an impossibility, a realization. Whether this saying is either of these or neither of them I do not know. But this is the story *before* the story, not the story the silence tells afterwards. To go forward, toward either the riddle's key or the impossibility, means to go by way of the story itself, in *loyalty*.

There are so many who may not, cannot, and do not write the story on a page to be read and interpreted. The old woman's tale is about (whatever else) a different kind of writing and a different kind of interpretation. Here the question of writing is a question of blood, and interpretation is the reading of it. It is also more, for there is the deciphering of what has not been written, even by the blood. But first things first: what kind of writing does blood do?

Other readers have elucidated very powerfully the connections between the terms of the story and the situations of women under the rule of the fathers.[1] There is an intricate web of relationships among gender, power, speech, writing, religion, body, marriage, creativity, blood, friendship, and memory. Start with one and you end up moving through them all, but always by a different route, according to where you begin, and why. The insistence upon the *connections* is fundamental to the ways of seeing that different expressions of feminism have brought.

Seeing connections often means trusting other eyes than your own, because your own have become so frozen. Oddly enough, one may learn to see, not by trying harder, but by closing one's eyes for a time, as it were, and *listening*—listening to speech that is born in loyalty to a different story.[2] The ear teaches the eye to see.

There are deep connections among different dimensions of suffering, alone and together. Dimensions of mind, body, spirit, family, community, class, race, and system refuse to remain discrete, but flow back and forth. There are patterns that emerge again and again across time or distance, however it is measured. Kneel down to trace the figure of the blood on the ground and you will recognize it; you will *remember* having seen such a pattern before. Still it will have a particularity, an individuality to it. To read the blood draws you into the whole fabric of suffering, but also into the singularity of the stained thread.

Because the Bible is the story I know best, it is from there that I have mostly learned the taxonomy of blood. There is the blood of murder, calling from the ground; the blood which carries the life; the blood of animals; the blood that gives evidence; the blood of the Passover; the blood of the river; the blood of sacrifice, upon the altar and the curtain and the mercy seat; the blood of birth; the monthly blood of women; the blood of battle; the blood of guilt; the blood of vengeance. There is the blood of family, of reconciliation, of innocence; the blood of visions and building cities. There is the blood of the covenant, of the cross, of the cup. There is the blood of the saints and the blood of the Lamb.

Blood is an alphabet of its own. The words it shapes, however, are not of a spoken language but a lived one. It has no absolute meaning of its own for humankind except one: it is always a trace of life, a sign that life has been this way. Writing may testify to an author, or to a world. Blood testifies to a life, both particular and connected. To say in what direction, how long ago, and why that life passed by here, however, requires more than the plain fact of blood. It requires loyalty—loyalty to follow, loyalty to the traces as they begin to spell a life, loyalty to the life that begins to take shape. It requires that the interpreter have the loyalty of presence.

The canvases, the old woman said, were hung in loyalty to the story. But there was an even greater loyalty, one which left even story-tellers speechless: the unswerving loyalty which hung a canvas without name or mark. This is the blank page, the all-absorbing page, which tells story beyond stories.

How can we talk about such a thing? Perhaps in the language of possibilities. Perhaps that is what the women read: how their own stories might have read had it not been for the webs of life signalled by the blood above their names. A story with no name can be anyone's story. A life that has not spilled into an ineradicable mark can be any life. It can also be no life, of course; that, too, is a possibility. It can signal denial, refusal, cowardice, hoarding. The white of snow is a cold white. White is the sterile color. The blank canvas can signal death, absence, bloodlessness.

In the empty canvas one may read stories of lives or deaths, then, but in particular one may read there a story of *escape*. The empty canvas is the sign of a life that has slipped away, somehow, from being inscribed in any frame, however beautiful, hung in any gallery, however honored. Who knows where such a life has gone? Escaped into what? Escaped at least from blood-writing, perhaps to be written in yet some other alphabet. Perhaps escaped even (it could be) into ink on a page! And maybe even to escape the snare of any kind of writing at all, the imprisonment of becoming the text which is fixed and repeated. It could be a great freedom, after all, to be *un*written, unavailable to memorization, available only to loyal memory.

This blank canvas is hung in loyalty, the old woman says, in unswerving and speech-defying loyalty to the story. But to which story? Is it to one story, one which is true, but simply hidden—a mysterious story, let us say, but not a story of Mystery? Perhaps it is loyalty to the story each woman reads as she stands before the unmarked sheet. Perhaps it is loyalty to the story of escape, which each might read and make her own. Perhaps it is loyalty to the story of stories being enacted and understood by women beyond what is written and read. Perhaps it is even loyalty to story itself, beyond telling or writing; loyalty to life unfolding in its own powers, surpassing and confounding every attempt to inscribe it. Whatever story it is, loyalty to it means to return to the place where its emblem hangs, and to be present there.

The "Blank Page" ends in silence. There is the silence told within the story itself, the silence of those who ponder before the unmarked cloth. There is the silence of the old story-teller, who does not return to speak in the end. With the end of her story her voice falls silent, too, so that the final word belongs to the tale, not the teller. There is the silence of the listeners within the story, and the silence of the reader. In the world of the story, this silence is the time of accounting, of revelation. It reveals who has spoken in loyalty, but also, who has listened in loyalty. Surely there is a loyalty of listening, too. There is a presence or absence in listening which makes all the difference. There is an inward telling of the listener, a telling of the imagination by which the hearer recreates the story in loyalty. There is an inward realization of the story as if it were memory, and this realization is a way of being present, abiding for a while.[3] The opposite is possible as well. One may choose disloyalty, refuse imagination, stand apart. One may choose the path of memorization rather than memory. The old woman does not say that loyalty is good and disloyalty bad. She does not say that loyalty means agreement or admiration or love. She only claims that loyalty is required if the silence is to speak.

There is a loyalty to the story, then, which goes beyond any written or spoken words. *Stories* are deeper than words. Stories are about blood, and the blood will speak only to those who remember.

WHAT IS WRITTEN, WHAT IS NOT

Dinesen's "The Caryatids" was first published in the collection of *Last Tales* (1975), although it had been written in 1934 and intended for the volume *Seven Gothic Tales*. It is subtitled "An Unfinished Gothic Tale" and it remained unfinished even in its later publication. The reasons were never clear. Dinesen would say only that "It is best that the story ends where it does. Best

102

for the characters and best for us. I did not dare continue" (in Langbaum 1975:220).

The story centers upon a husband and wife, Philippe and Childerique. Unknown to each other, they are in fact brother and sister. Her mother, Sophie, and his father had been lovers years ago, before Philippe's family had left France for Canada. The father had died without sharing the truth, so upon returning to the ancestral home, Philippe had no way of knowing that the young woman he would marry was really his sister. Childerique's mother had died many years before, also without leaving word. Her "father" had remarried, and the stepmother had borne a son—a "brother" to whom Childerique felt powerfully attracted. Toward her "brother" she felt as to a lover; toward her husband she felt as to a "brother." Her younger "brother," however, was drawn toward Simkie, a young gypsy widow who lived in the forest.

Simkie was known as the mill witch. She and all the gypsies in the region were full of secrets and magic. They knew the ways of snakes, darkness, curses, and of reading the past and future. It was said that once they had cursed old Father Bernhard because of his interference with their ways. Although he had been no scholar, he suddenly became obsessed with reading the scriptures. Just before his disappearance, he was found one day sitting beside the market road as pigs were being driven by. He had become convinced that these were the possessed Gadarene swine whose devils now would infest him and drive him into the mountains to cut himself with stones. "I said nothing to him," recounted the one who had found him. "What can one answer to things out of the Holy Book?" (111)

One day, however, Philippe discovered an old letter Sophie had written in which the truth was set down. In anguish he read of their true relationship, and finally decided that for the sake of Childerique's honor and sanity, and his own love for her, he would tell no one of the discovery. Philippe burned the letter and sealed the secret within himself.

Childerique and her "brother" come to a crisis. He announces that he will marry Simkie in three days. Childerique tries to change his mind, and insists that she, too, can teach him dances, darkness, and magic, but he turns away. She decides that she must go to the witch's mill and confront her. What unfolds is a remarkable encounter.

Childerique accuses Simkie of bewitching "brother" with her magic and demands his release. Simkie insists that such things are not easily undone, and describes what steps must be taken, what Childerique herself must risk. Childerique hesitates out of uncertainty, and also fear. To convince her, Simkie offers to show her magic.

Down by the mill, Simkie summons the magic of the water wheel, "which is the most honest of all magics." She sets the wheel free to turn and orders Childerique to watch what the water shows. At first it is a strange vision, wheeling red sparks coming together. At length it forms into a scene of primeval forest where the estate now stands. Childerique is ecstatic, powerfully transported. "She no longer asked herself what it all meant, or why the gypsy was showing it to her. She felt only a deep ecstasy about this new world opened to her" (146).

What appears at last is a scene from the past. Childerique sees from a distance her mother meeting in the woods with a man she takes to be Sophie's husband, her supposed father. In the beauty of their meeting, and in her own rapture at meeting the mother she had not known, she cannot see the man's real identity, Philippe's father. She sees in the two the image of herself and Philippe, but does not understand how literally true it is. Childerique is overwhelmed by the sweetness of the magic and feels herself deepened and changed, and also renewed in her affection for Philippe. When the visions come to an end, Simkie says, "I have shown you true pictures" (148).

Simkie has indeed shown true pictures, but her magic extracted what Childerique could not know. The charm was to "turn the heart of your brother, your father's son, entirely away from the woman whom he now loves, and thinks of as his wife" (142). The charm, that is, had actually been spoken against Childerique and Philippe, not the "brother" and Simkie. The tale breaks off as Childerique returns home hoping to embrace her husband, only to find that he is strangely distant, preoccupied, looking off into the sky. This is as far as the story goes.

This is a story of texts and "texts," reading and "reading," and both the insistence and refusal of interpretation. There is the Holy Book and a cursed interpreter. From the hand of a dead woman comes a letter which has the power to undo everything. There is the text of taboo, and the text of genealogy which must be read correctly so the taboo is not broken. There are texts of feeling and attraction, texts of intuition. There are texts of social fabric, culture, religion; texts of body, otherness, animals. There are texts of charms, intentions, visions, water, relationship. Some of them are written, most are not. Some of them are interpreted in a conscious way, some unconsciously, while still others are refused interpretation. These latter ones are the most powerful, for they themselves become the interpreters of the rest without being seen.

The interplay of these texts is finally impossible to chronicle, but the oppositions point repeatedly to the question of what makes a text and what textuality might really be. What appears to be fixed, stable, repeatable, referable, is disclosed as fluid, unstable, singular, elusive. What is "written" is repeatedly overturned by the "unwritten," by what cannot be written, or has not been allowed to be written.

> Out of an old, tortoise-shell box, which opened by the touch of a spring, a packet of letters, tied together with a pale blue ribbon, came into his hand. They were love letters, written by a lady to her lover, by Childerique's mother to his father. Afterwards he remembered how he had, after the first glance, got up to destroy them, when his eyes had been caught by his own name . . . (123)

> He made a heap of all the letters together with the same ribbon, struck a light and watched them flame up and come to ashes upon the cold fireplace.
> So Childerique was his father's child . . . (123-4)

> He sat for a long time in the room, to make up his mind . . . In the end, before he left the room again, he had sealed his mouth and his heart forever; she should never know that anything had been changed between them. He thought: It would bring down all the world . . . (126)

On the side of the "written" stand estate, law, scripture, lineage, authorized history, paternity, class, fields, male order upheld by women, social role, public knowledge, and clear boundaries—between good and evil, religion and magic, settled and wild, animal and human. On the side of the "unwritten" stand mill, desire, water, the unauthorized, order subverted by women, classlessness, forest, fluid roles, hidden and secret knowledge, and transgressed boundaries of all kinds.

Between the two stands interpretation. In some ways it is a work of holding together two worlds which are straining apart; in some ways it is keeping apart two worlds rushing together to overwhelm each other. The "written" is revealed as an attempt to *declare* what is, and to have it be so. It holds the power of official names, lists, emblems, law, distinguishing titles, category, the given and assumed, and it wields that power to declare a written world. The "unwritten" is revealed as an attempt to *discover* what is and communicate with it. It holds the power of secret names, formulas, magical signs, desire, connection, vitality, the hidden and surprising, and it wields that power to maintain and expand the places of discovery and communication. The "written" attempts alternately to deny and control the "unwritten." It threatens some and negotiates some. It circumscribes and erases, denies and acknowledges, binds and looses. The "unwritten" resists in its own way. It must both refuse to be named and allow itself to be named; it must deny the authority but recognize the power. Sometimes it must frighten and sometimes calm, sometimes stay within the boundaries, sometimes overflow them; mystify and demystify, enchant and release, stay near and travel far.

In the world of this story, the "written" is opposed by the "unwritten." It is resisted, subverted, and finally undone, and interpretation is the place where this dance of conflict is enacted. Because it is in interpretation that the "written" makes its attempt to circumscribe the "unwritten," so it is in interpretation that the "unwritten" resists. The effect of its resistance is to transform, and even reverse the intention and meaning of the written. It turns the written back upon itself as its own enemy, its own undoing.

Through an interpretation which is unaware of its role, often even unaware of being interpretation at all, the "unwritten" works its spell. Interpretation is revealed as haunted, as if possessed by ghosts or spirits. Words and meaning fly apart and are carried through the air by invisible forces. The words may belong to the written, but meaning belongs to the unwritten. The unseen lives inside the mirror and disguises itself as the seen, and so everything is reversed. The "written" is revealed as an inscribed denial which refers to its unwritten opposite. Just as the watercolorist leaves the white areas blank, and "paints" those areas by painting around them (creating a negative shape), so the "written" paints around the "unwritten."

In the world of this story the spaces which are unwritten are anything but empty. They are the places where deeper power lives, where the "more" of living experience refuses to be ruled by the "less" of what can be written. The written is the place of words, but the unwritten is the place where meaning is found. These unwritten spaces pull with the power of a star's gravity, drawing everything into orbit around themselves. It is around the unwritten spaces that the "texts" rotate. Instead of being what is fixed and central while the unwritten is marginal, the "texts" are revealed as uncentered and marginal themselves. They are captured by the power of the unwritten center. The lived world is stronger than the authorized world. It is around the lived world that the texts of authorization revolve as lesser satellites, although a Ptolemaic imagination believes otherwise.

In the world of this story the relationship between written and unwritten, then, is reversed or inverted like the famous silhouettes which show either a kiss or a vase depending upon how you look. Rather than being formless and chaotic, the unwritten is full of forms and orders. Rather than being senseless and meaningless, the unwritten is the super-abundance of meaning and multiple senses. It resists being *disordered* through writing. The unwritten is the space between the letters that holds them apart and prevents them from flowing together into meaninglessness, into an ultimate triumph of ink which erases by flooding the page.

In a strange reversal, narrative in particular is saved not by being written, but by the blank page, the empty space that marks the limit of the written. The written narrative is saved by the writing coming to an end, so that the *story* can be. The words and the story are not the same. The story has its own reality which does not depend upon this writing or that telling. A particular narrative must be memorized, but a story can be remembered.[4] And so through the unwritten story, the written narrative is saved as well. It is *about* a story, but is not the story itself. Only because it is *about* a story can it be a written narrative, but the writing neither exhausts the story nor replaces it. The writing is an *occasion* of the story, a crystallization, through which the story may happen. So the writing is saved from becoming nothing in its attempt to become everything. It is saved by pointing away from itself, even against its will. The "unwritten" is like the silence which precedes the beginning of the telling and thus makes it the beginning, and like the silence which makes the end the end. It is upon silence that the telling is superimposed, and only with the return of the concluding silence can the story finally be.

HAUNTED INTERPRETATION

Interpretation in this world is haunted by the unwritten, which undoes, but also secretly saves and sustains both writing and its interpretation. There are two distinct kinds of possibility for such haunted interpretation. The first is an interpretation which is haunted and does not, cannot, or will not acknowledge it. It does not see the page itself, the life, the story—the unwritten— that makes the writing possible. It does not see the power and super-abundance of meaning which writing attempts to circum- scribe, but is enchanted by the beaten drum of words. The house of interpretation is then haunted by ghosts of denial, which like any good ghosts announce themselves in ways that may be alarming, mystifying, annoying, terrifying, humorous, or simply embarrassing. The ghosts take up their residence in the very words of interpretation as in portraits along the wall. One moment the interpreter is gazing calmly upon the known and fixed face of some venerable ancestor word, and the next moment discovers a strange face staring back, like the interpreter's own face twisted in a carnival mirror.[5] As such an interpreter my words turn on me as a caricature of me and reveal what I did not intend to reveal, indeed, what I did not suppose I knew. The ghosts rehearse again and again the unwritten secrets from which writing has turned, from which interpretation has turned.

There is a second possibility for haunted interpretation. It does not escape the haunting, for in this sort of world nothing does. Rather than escape, it engages. It is, however, a different engagement than Childerique's. She went to the mill witch to assert her own claim. She was the one, after all, who had insisted that she knew both the world of the established and the world of the magical; she too, could teach magic, she said. But what she declared and what she really knew were not the same. She read the waters as if she knew how to read them. She read Simkie's attestation of the truth as if she knew how it was true. She read as if there were no *difference* between them. That is, she read as if the very fact which had brought her to the mill in the first place did not matter: that Simkie was *different* from her. Childerique's interpretation was undone because of the denial of difference, of otherness. She declared meaning and believed her own declaration, as if what she understood could be substituted for what she had seen and heard. But the story was not limited to her own telling of it. The story had its own reality which could not be encompassed by a monologue. Simkie knew the power of the unwritten story to undo the written through interpretation which denied difference.

The denial of difference may take the shape, as it does in this tale, of an interpretation which simply asserts itself over the unwritten, assumes the privilege of interpretation, disposes of the unwritten as if it were part of the written. It may also take the shape of surrender, giving over, giving up interpretation to the unwritten, as if one could understand simply by being silent or acquiescing. This would seem to be the solution of the younger "brother." In "Caryatids," however, the absence of a continuation and conclusion denies us the opportunity to see if such a logic unfolds any farther. Both solutions—assertion and silence—are in any case univocal, and therefore both are denials of difference.

Instead, this second possibility for haunted interpretation insists upon the difference. The written and the unwritten are different; they are Other to one another. Although standing between the two, interpretation stands closer to the place of the written, the place where Otherness is turned into writing, into a narrative, into a text, with all the inevitable misperception and miswriting. Nevertheless this interpretation insists upon the necessity of the Otherness, the misperception, the misunderstanding. It is a debt of humility which must be paid; it is the cost of dialogue. My misperception is a confession of my particularity, a confession of the true state of affairs. In one sense this is the same as the essential Otherness of another person. The other person always eludes, escapes, and goes beyond me. The other person will always be more and different from what I perceive and inscribe. Nevertheless, we can engage one another, learn about one another and ourselves—but only through affirmation of the Otherness. This is the price of engagement, the price of dialogue. And dialogue is the essence of interpretation. "The most important acts, constitutive of self-consciousness, are determined by their relationship to another consciousness (a thou) . . . The very being of [a person] (both internal and external) is a *profound communication. To be* means to *communicate*" (Tsvetan Todorov 1984:96; italics mine). This is the voice of Mikhail Bakhtin and his dialogical principle. "Life is dialogical by its very nature. To live means to engage in dialogue, to question, to listen, to answer" (Todorov 1984:97).

Dialogue, then, is the discourse of difference. It rests upon difference; it requires it and explores it. It is founded upon difference, and supposes that difference is necessary for the partners of the dialogue to come to themselves. Difference makes dialogue possible, but not difference alone. Dialogue presupposes likeness or identity as well. If there is only difference there is no dialogue, and if there is only identity there is also no dialogue. How can one describe the relationship of difference and identity which makes dialogue possible? One possibility is to call it the relationship of metaphor.

The Other and I stand in a metaphoric relationship, as metaphors to one another and of one another. Metaphor depicts a relationship of identity-in-difference and difference-in-identity. It produces meaning only where the distance between the two terms is not collapsed, where it is remembered that the terms brought together are *different*. The difference pushes apart, the identity pulls together, and in the space held open between them the meaning of metaphor happens.[6]

There is a tension here which must not be resolved. Insofar as I interpret the Other through my own understanding and my own story (my pole of the metaphor), I misinterpret. Yet without this misinterpretation, which is the root of metaphor, no space for meaning opens up *between*. No scandal of meaning happens—no scandal of difference where identity was presumed, no scandal of identity where difference was presumed.

In the world of "The Caryatids" meaning and scandal are deeply bound to one another, bound together as metaphors for one another. Scandal lies in the between places; it is the unwritten meaning of each relationship. The "written" is the literalized metaphor which has lost its meaning because it has lost the real relationship of metaphor; it is the scandal of identity and difference turned upside down. The flight from scandal in the world of this story brings about (at least as far as the story goes) the very downfall it sought to avoid by fleeing.

What then is the work of haunted interpretation in this second possibility? It talks *with* the "ghosts" of the unwritten, not about them. It invokes the ghosts, and questions them. It asks the ghosts about themselves, and invites their questions in return. It *speaks* to the ghosts about themselves, and confesses itself. Haunted interpretation refuses literalization of itself or the Other and reaches toward the scandals of difference and identity which live in the space between.

The dialogue between the interpreter and what is haunting reaches no resolution, just as the terms of metaphor do not. A metaphor's first term establishes the field of meanings, the constellation of images, the known. The second term violates the boundaries of that field, disarranges the shape of the constellation, and calls the known into question. But the process continues. The second term is also put to the test. It, too, has a field of meanings, images, and identity, and the first term must now be numbered among them; and so the scandal flows back in the other direction. There is no point of equilibrium, no synthesis. The known becomes unknown, the unknown known, and back again. The stronger the metaphor, the deeper the reversal of identity and difference. The stronger the metaphor, the more powerful the mutual transformation.

This, then, is the second possibility for interpretation under the terms of this story. It is interpretation as the exegesis of the scandal of meaning which happens when the written and unwritten come face to face as metaphors for one another.

TRACES OF LIFE, SCANDAL OF METAPHOR

We have considered here two stories of interpretation which point away from the written text and point toward another kind of exegesis. In the first it was a dialogue of story and silence, blood and blankness, a dialogue which one enters by way of loyalty. In the second it was a dialogue of the "written" and the "unwritten," denial and desire, enacting a perpetual drama of the scandalous reversal of difference and identity. Although each story has its distinct identity, there are also some shared possibilities for interpretation under their shared sign.

For both stories, interpretation becomes an exegesis of the traces of life. Such an exegesis looks to the place where the ink ends and the blood begins. Edmond Jabès (1972) wrote, "Mark the first page of the book with a red marker. For, in the beginning, the wound is invisible." Ink is a sign of blood. It is a sign of something else inscribed elsewhere which is not written in words, but enacted. To turn to *that* means to turn from script to drama. To say that human experience is story does not necessarily privilege the story which is written or spoken. Those stories are themselves abstractions from the drama which is embodied, enacted, lived. Silence is not the absence of drama, only the absence of a story-teller; the blank page is not the absence of drama, only the absence of its writing. Drama is what happens and who does it. Drama lives and dies. Drama is blood, not ink.

As the written narrative depicts story, story depicts drama—but at a distance, as a fiction of the past. The written story is fixed, closed, even if it is utterly ambiguous. It is closed in one sense because its language has been chosen and set and may not be added or subtracted. The words may be questioned, compared, inspected, and analyzed, but they are the terms which must be dealt with. It is closed in another sense because it confers a "pastness" to what it says. Even if the subject is the future, as a *story* its narration comes after. The told story may avoid the first closure, but not the second. The enacted drama which has not yet been distanced into *a* story, however, remains a theater of possibility, a theater of the present in which the future is shaped.[7] The time of drama is now. The events are in the present. The characters are here. The *story* which fixes them as part of the irremediable past is only one possibility. *This* drama in front of us may be *that* story, or *another*, or *another*. It has characters, events, words, actions, and things, but what links them and arranges them is not yet given. The *story* which tells what the drama is, is not yet closed.

An exegesis of the traces of life takes up where the ink ends and the blood begins. It asks about drama. It asks whose blood is there, whose blood is not, and why. It asks whose blood is considered beautiful, costly, and what makes it so. It asks about the taxonomy of blood, and the economy of blood. An exegesis of the traces of life is about the present and presence. It can only take place where the traces themselves are found. There is no book which one can carry anywhere, and no story which may be re-told any time. One must be where and when the blood is, for this is an exegesis done in loyalty to the drama itself, which is far beyond what has been written or told.[8]

This exegesis of the traces of life, therefore, asks about the future more than the past; that is the direction in which the blood flows. It recognizes that interpretation inevitably transforms the drama into story (and perhaps into telling and writing), and that this story shapes the future. Such interpretation takes responsibility for the future the story builds. Texts need nothing, stories need nothing, not even interpretation. Blood needs the future.

There is a second possibility for interpretation which these stories share. In these stories interpretation is exegesis of the scandal of metaphor. "To understand oneself before the text" is a famous phrase describing a culminating moment of interpretation. "To understand oneself before the Other" would be an appropriate rephrasing for these stories. Such an understanding happens through the dialogue of metaphors which never merge with one another in identity, and never break with one another in utter difference.

The special warning for interpretation is that the discovery and recognition of identity and difference is a process of deep contradiction. What I suppose to be my identity with the other, and difference from the other, is itself a kind of denial. It is part of my strategy—however unintended or well-meaning—to "write" myself through "writing" the other, while maintaining the prerogatives of writing for my own. The dialogue of metaphor which characterizes the engagement with an Other must keep about it, therefore, the strongest sense of the dialectical. Where I suppose our identity to lie, there we must talk most deeply about difference; where I suppose our difference to be, there we must talk most deeply about identity. I must look closely to see if my own blood is not where I suppose the marks of your blood to be. My own shadowy blood, perhaps flowing in a different direction, may also stain the ground upon which we both stand. When I suppose it is my own life whose marks I trace with my finger, I must squint my eyes and see if my life is not spelled there with the letters of your name, and written in the blood of your life.

Where to stand, how to begin, how to look, how to hear, how to ask, how to refrain from asking, how to depart, how to keep silence, how to repeat, how to interpret? Not here, where the ink is. There.

6

THE
EXEGESIS
OF
PRESENCE

WHO IS THE THIRD?

Who is the third who walks always beside you?
— T. S. Eliot, "The Wasteland"

There is a book of photographs by Andre Kertesz called *On Reading*. The images, assembled over more than fifty years of work from Europe to the Americas to Asia, are all images of people reading. Two Japanese women in kimonos sit side by side on a train, each holding a book and gazing at the open page. An old man with a magnifier hunches over a New York book stall, holds an open volume close to his face and squints. A woman in a Manila market squats in the passageway, holding before her the remains of a crumpled newspaper. Three young Hungarian boys, two without shoes, lean close together as they sit against a wall, their eyes fixed upon the open book held in the middle boy's lap. In a high room lined with books, a well-dressed man with spats on his shoes stands half-way up a ladder examining an open volume in his hands, while two end mirrors reflect the room endlessly. In the final photograph, an old woman of the Hospice de Beaune sits wrapped in her shawl, covered in bedclothes, propped up in her bed by thick pillows. In her hands she holds an open book and her eyes are fixed upon the page.

How different are the places, times, and people of these photographs. And yet in every one something is repeated: there is a page and a reader. Crowds, vistas, traffic, business, solitude—whatever streams of life flow around the scene, they divide upon this rock of page and reader.

The images are all mysterious in a way. They are mysterious because of their eloquent failure. There is a mystery at hand which cannot be photographed, and the image which succeeds only does so by the grace and honesty of its failure. The successful image holds before us the most common bread of experience in such a way that the *fact* of its mystery may be seen—not the *content* of the mystery, the mystery itself, but the simple presence of it which cannot be seen. Call it a kind of sacramental failure, the same failure by which the bread and cup do not become extraordinary and transcendent, but by which grace comes nonetheless to be eaten and drunk. The photos display, one could say, the "outward and visible signs of an inward and invisible grace."

It is the nature of a photograph to provoke questions about what cannot be seen. The etched moment is the intersection of many stories, and is both too much and too little to regard for long without asking about the past and future of the moment. Too much, because it testifies to that deafening "roar which lives on the other side of silence," to recall George Eliot's famous words. Too little, because moments have meaning and significance—or even plain intelligibility—according to the story in which they occur.

Kertesz' work was criticized by his American editors: "Your pictures talk too much." Perhaps what the editors meant was that the images refused to lose their particularity and pass over into a purely formal beauty. Resisting abstraction they remained pictures of life displaying itself, life speaking about life. The child in the doorway sprawled over a pile of torn papers reading the comics does not become "everychild" but seems more and more *that* child: a presence, not a metaphor; an incarnation, not a form. Perhaps what the editors really meant was that the images make the *viewer* "talk too much"! The images push toward telling a story, or asking questions. What is written? Why there and then? Who is this? What is happening? Each photograph seems so ripe with untold stories that it is easy to forget where the stories really are. The stories are in the viewer. The silent photograph pulls hard upon stories untold and unknown, stories which were unimagined until this picture came.

Take the pictures together, nevertheless, and a singular image does begin to form. Look at each picture and there is only those two, reader and text; look at them together as they are going away, however, and there is more than just those two. Something else is there which is neither one. A mystery is there, and the presence of that mystery is what each picture is about—what reading is about. Seen in the sanctuary of the frame it appears that what each person reads is scripture. It makes no difference that the text may be a letter, a novel, the comics, or a newspaper. It may or may not be scripture in the usual sense, but whatever scripture is, it could be read in just such a way. Whatever the experience of reading scripture is—let us say it in the plural: whatever experiences of reading scripture are—these photos could be among them.

A reader, a text, a hidden presence, . . . look at the picture and there are only two, but in every one, between the two, there is a third. Who is the third?

ON THE ROAD TO EMMAUS

> Now on that same day two of them were going to a village called Emmaus, about seven miles from Jerusalem, and talking with each other about all these things that had happened. While they were talking and discussing, Jesus himself came near and went with them, but their eyes were kept from recognizing him.

On the same day that they had heard an idle tale of angels, two disciples walked toward a small town which no one can find anymore. Even if the tale had been idle there was enough to talk about. There were events and reports of the recent days: a meal, a darkened journey to the Mount of Olives, the arrest, the torture and interrogation, the sentencing, the execution. There had been the sun's eclipse, the soldier's strange confession, the crowd's dispersal, all of which the people of Jesus had watched from a distance. Then there had been the council member who, for reasons of his own, had the courage to ask for the body and do the decent thing. There had been the sabbath rest, according to the commandment. The irony could scarcely be deeper. A day to remember the creation of the world, and to remember the mighty hand that brought Israel out of Egypt. Add to these events the sayings full of echoes, sayings with the sound of caverns stretching room after hidden room; talk about thrones and realms, feasting and judgment, scripture and swords. They discussed "all these things," and whatever else of the story they knew that might make these things into some kind of shape, some kind of sense, some kind of story with an ending, happy or otherwise. What does it mean to "discuss" but this: to bring events into words, and words into a story, and a story into a world of stories. But notice how the narrator does not say just what all these things might be, or should be. When the time comes, the disciples will speak for themselves and reveal themselves by the story they tell. In the same way, the readers who care to consider "all these things" disclose who they are, and how they have thought and discussed. What must one recount, what must one recite, what must one discuss in order to bring "all these things" into words, into story, in *the* story?

The setting for the episode is completed in a single sentence. There remains only the question of the event which propels the story forward—the conflict or problem which draws things into a plot. The appearance of Jesus upon the road and the holding of the disciples' eyes from recognition announce the theme of what will follow. The disciples are kept from knowing their companion's identity; the story will tell us how they learned not only who this companion is, but who he was all along. Yet a second story is unfolding at the same time. There on the road the one story forks into two: one about disciples hearing and seeing, and one about readers reading. The disciples enact one plot while the reader enacts another. For the disciples the tests will be put as tests of faith for those who have at hand only the stories they know and can put together. They

118

must argue and tell them into a world, different from the one they had previously woven. From the beginning they must tell through to the end.

The reader is tested differently. For the reader the task will be to read backwards, from end to beginning, from the future of all these things toward their past. As we shall see, one problem is as great as the other, and the story must be told backwards and forwards, and back again. Only by telling from the beginning through the middle to the end, can one tell the story. Only by telling from the end to the middle to the beginning can one understand, and begin to tell again.

> And he said to them, "What are you discussing with each other while you walk along?" They stood still, looking sad. Then one of them, whose name was Cleopas, answered him, "Are you the only stranger in Jerusalem who does not know the things that have taken place there in these days?" He asked them, "What things?"

A stranger asks a question of the disciples, who apparently consider it rather foolish and self-evident. From where do you have to come not to know the events in Jerusalem? And if one does not know, where do you start to tell the story? There is more to it than that, of course. To tell what they think they know, the disciples must say what they believe. One can discuss and recount events, even put them end to end, but to shape them into a story is a public act of faith. It requires choosing *one* place from which to see and speak, one place from which to believe as long as the story lasts. The confession becomes even more public when the story must include the teller among the characters. The teller is, of course, *always* among the characters in the drama of telling, but sometimes the drama allows at least a mask or curtain, a disguise or role. Here there is no place to hide. To tell about these things they must tell a story about themselves. They must confess themselves.

The reader knows what the disciples do not. What the disciples will answer, therefore, must be wrong because of what they do not know: Jesus' resurrection. And because they do not know this resurrection, they do not know who Jesus was and is. Thus they are revealed not as narrators of their own story, but characters in the story another tells. Even if every event is recounted correctly and every word reported truly, they are undercut by a hidden presence. "But we had hoped," they will say. That is, "we had told ourselves this story."

The disciples, however, have known what the reader has not. They have known Jesus. Their eyes must be held to *keep* from recognizing him until the time is right. For the reader the situation is different. Supernatural intervention is not needed to keep recognition at bay, but to bring it about. The reader has known Jesus only through the story, and by what the author has chosen to hide and reveal. If the problem for the disciples is one of recognizing the Jesus they know, the problem for the reader is knowing the Jesus one has never, nor can ever, meet. What kind of knowledge is this? How does it happen? How is it possible to speak about such things? The disciples will tell the story wrongly. The reader will read the story—how?

> He asked them "What things?" They answered him, "The things about Jesus of Nazareth, who was a prophet mighty in deed and word before God and all the people, and how our chief priests and leaders handed him over to be condemned to death and crucified him. But we had hoped that he was the one to redeem Israel."

The disciples somehow answer together, an odd thing to do. People only answer together when they know such words by heart. Who was Jesus? Let us recite: a prophet mighty in deed and word before God and all the people. That is what the narrator and various characters have said all along. Later, when the apostles will preach empowered by the Holy Spirit, they still will say such things.[1] What happened to him? Let us recite: handed over, condemned, crucified. How can this follow? It always follows, or something like it, for that is what the ancestors did with prophets (Luke 6:23). Besides, Jesus had already been taken to the brow of one hill and escaped (4:29-30), so it should have been clear from the start. There was no escape from the last hill.

Handed over, condemned, crucified. All in the passive voice; acted upon, not acting. How could one have seen that what was being done *to* him, was somehow being done *by* him—that *he* was the one whose story this was? How could one understand that handed over, condemned, and crucified are not the great contradiction of "mighty in word and deed"? But this is the way the disciples know to tell the story. To be handed over, condemned, crucified, in the story world they live in, is the end of mighty words and mighty deeds by mightier words and deeds. Condemnation to death is a stronger word than the prophet's word. Crucifixion is a stronger deed. So with the end of mighty words and deeds hope ends.

"But we had hoped that he was the one to redeem Israel." In the world the disciples narrate, hope is founded upon power. Hope is the interpretation of power. Mighty words and deeds are not only performed; as power they are read and interpreted. They are interpreted as signs of the future. Thus to interpret them means telling a story about the future which fits with such mighty words and deeds. Power is read as a promise. Power is read as the presence of the future, which fulfills the story begun in these words and deeds. This is what hope means in such a world.

But then despair is the same. It too is the interpretation of power. Power is read as the threat of a future and the presence of that future. Hope and despair alike are thus tied to the interpretation of power; whether one hopes or despairs depends on which words and deeds prove mightiest. Presence is bound to power, and recognized in power. Jesus is real when he is powerful; when he has no more mighty words and deeds, the story of Jesus is over, and the story of the future belongs to whoever does.

The disciples, then, tell the truth, but they tell it "slant." Jesus had indeed done and said mighty things, and had been a prophet before God and the people. Their interpretation, however, was of the wrong text, as Jesus will shortly reveal. They have read the text of power, supposing that this is where the future is written, whether for hope or despair. But there is a different way of reading available. In this reading, the text of power is really a testimony to the past. The future is present in a different way, as suffering which will be redeemed. To read of the future, then, one must turn to the text of suffering. "Blessed

are you who are poor. . . . Blessed are you who are hungry
now. . . . Blessed are you who weep now. . . . Blessed are you
when people hate you. . . ."

> "Yes, and beside all this, it is now the third day since these
> things took place. Moreover, some women of our group
> astounded us. They were at the tomb early this morning, and
> when they did not find his body there, they came back and
> told us that they had indeed seen a vision of angels who said
> that he was alive. Some of those who were with us went to
> the tomb and found it just as the women had said; but they
> did not see him."

The story of Jesus comes to an end with the word "crucified." Beyond that it is the story of Jesus' community. Some
women of the community came back from the tomb, the disciples say, with "a vision of angels who said that [Jesus] was
alive." That isn't quite correct, and the mistelling is revealing.
Mary Magdalene, Joanna, Mary the mother of James, and other
women who went to the tomb were confronted with two figures
in dazzling clothes who said much more than that Jesus was
alive. They asked the women why they sought the living among
the dead. They said "he has *risen*." They told the women to
remember what Jesus had said to them: the Human One must
be handed over, crucified, and rise again on the third day.[2]
The women *did* remember Jesus' words, and all this, the text
insists, they had told to the rest (Luke 24:5-10). All of this, of
course, is dismissed as an idle tale, one not worth repeating
correctly it would seem. But it is strange that the disciples would
say they were astounded and proceed to mistell the story.

Why seek the living among the dead? It is another of Luke's
many ironic jokes.[3] The irony is directed not toward the events
in question, but toward the people. Irony is about perception,
that is, interpretation. Irony attacks an interpretation indirectly,
enclosing it, reversing its signs, making it into the opposite of
what it claims to be. Irony presents the reversal as a *fait accom-
pli*, without argument, all at once. There is in such irony an
implicit narrative present. It is a deep narrative of one who is
wise and one who is foolish, of one who sees rightly and one
who sees wrongly, of one who knows the real story and one

who only supposes. Such an irony depends upon surprise, a surprise which throws a person into confusion because suddenly one's ability to give a coherent account of oneself and the world had been undone. It works not because a story has been argued or shown to be mistaken, but because one's own fundamental interpretive world has been *experienced* in eclipse. The announcement is about Jesus, but the irony is about the visitors to the tomb.

It was inevitable that the women's account would not be believed. They spoke from inside a story which had died and not yet from inside the one which was alive. They could not yet command the irony by which the others would experience their story eclipsed. Yet the dazzling strangers did give explicit directions to the women about how to begin to reshape the story and understand. "Remember how he told you. . . ." There was a starting place available to all of them, and it had been told to them, and they knew it was there. What they had heard and seen was not wrong, and what had happened could be trusted. But the memories had been told into the wrong story.

Nevertheless, the story could be healed from within the story; within the story there was enough. In spite of all this the other apostles do not begin there. They rush off to the tomb where nothing awaits them. They rush to an absence instead of memory. The disciples on the road, therefore, mistell the story as they must. They can only tell a story in which Jesus is still a body, missing or otherwise, and the subject of only passive verbs—handed over, condemned, crucified—not yet of the active one—he has risen.

As their speech comes to an end the next step of the ironic reversal is prepared. First there had been the question about the stranger being the only one who did not know what had happened, when in fact he was the only one who did. Next there had been the statement of how wrong their hope had been, when in fact it was correct, and even better than they had known. Now, at the speech's conclusion, comes the recognition (by the reader, at least) that they had even been told exactly where to look, and had gone exactly in the wrong direction. The story continues with the stranger on the road who knows nothing speaking more like angels than the angels, and more like Jesus than Jesus.

SUFFERING, NECESSITY, AND THE JUST ONE

> Then he said to them, "Oh how foolish you are and how slow of heart to believe all that the prophets have declared! Was it not necessary that the Messiah should suffer these things and then enter into his glory?" Then beginning with Moses and all the prophets, he interpreted to them the things about himself in all the scriptures.

The women's story had not been foolish. The stranger had not been foolish. Even they themselves had not been foolish in their hope, except in the reasons for it. They had, however, been guilty of folly in another way. Folly has to do with judgment, decisions, actions, interpretation—interpretation in particular. It implies a certain kind of false reading: not simply a mistaken one (what reading is not mistaken?) but a thoughtless or forgetful one. What makes such a reading is failure to recognize that forgetting is at the heart of telling a story. To make a story one chooses both to remember and forget—to remember by telling, to forget by not telling. But what is forgotten does not, therefore, become unreal. Foolishness forgets, believes that only what it tells is real, and is undone by its forgetfulness. It breaks upon the power of the forgotten. Wisdom, by contrast, remembers its forgetfulness, and is always seeking the blessing of the forgotten, invoking the forgotten, restoring the forgotten to the story. "Remember . . . ," say the angels.

But to do so threatens the possibility of telling a story. A story *must* forget in order to be told, for that is the nature of a story. The stranger turns the disciples from what they themselves can remember and tell to a different kind of recollection: scripture. Scripture is not memory in the usual sense, because it is writing. Apart from writing, we only know what we can say. With writing we can know more than anyone can remember. With writing, the past becomes more than the sphere of memory. It acquires an independence, a power, an ability to shape and reshape. Writing establishes an "otherness," both of itself and of what it is about. It implies a transcendence and points away from immanence; it testifies to discontinuity. With writing the past retains the power to erupt in the immediate present, even to overturn the remembered story.[4] Writing has a subversive potential, therefore. It has the power to subvert what is told, to press a claim for which there may be no other voice present, the power to *eclipse*. The women remembered but could be dismissed. What is written cannot be unwritten.

To have a *scripture*, therefore, means to establish a permanent conflict, dialectic, and dialogue. A community with a scripture lives within the conflict of what is remembered and what is written, what is told and what is inscribed. It lives with a past which is not one with the present but an other to the present.

Because it is written, scripture can do what telling cannot. It does not need to have characteristics which telling must; it can disorder, leap, complexify, frustrate, bore, meander. It can be endlessly incoherent, and even lie unread through generations, because coherence is not the job of writing, but of memory.

There is, however, an edge where scripture and memory meet. Scripture is not *only* written; it is also remembered. It is taken up into memory and told as memory, with the necessary remembering and forgetting that all telling entails. It is incorporated into other stories and vice versa. That is to say, it is *interpreted*. This is the fundamental work of its interpretation: not the deciphering of this passage or that, but the telling of scripture into a story-world. Standing between what is written and what is told, interpretation turns to the scripture to recollect what the present story has forgotten, and turns to the story to shape the forgotten and remembered together into a renewed world.

The two strangers in dazzling clothes had pointed to two facts and two ways of apprehending them: Jesus' absence, which the women can see, and Jesus' words, which the women remember. Instead of a present prophet with mighty acts and words, they spoke of a risen Human One whose words are remembered. The more extraordinary but less dazzling stranger on the road pointed in a third direction: the things about Jesus which had been written in all the scriptures, beginning with Moses and the prophets. He turned them toward the place where scripture and memory meet, and began to speak it into story in a different way. The words he chose for the force of his story are strong ones. He speaks of the unfolding of "all these things" in their seeming contradiction—the mighty words and deeds, handed over, condemned, crucified—in terms of *suffering*, and the suffering he calls *necessary*.

"Was it not necessary that the Messiah should suffer these things?" The form of the question, followed by the breaking off of dialogue and return to narration, provides another kind of irony, one turned upon the reader. Until now it has been the disciples who did not know, who were foolish and slow to believe "all that the prophets have declared." In the shift from dialogue to narration, the plot that the disciples follow and the one the reader follows cross. The reader, who knew Jesus was risen and who the stranger was, is now removed from the role of insider, while the disciples have the scriptures revealed to them. What is taught before the reader's eyes (but out of the reader's hearing) is not simply a discourse about scripture, but the unveiling of the *necessity* at work in it. The reader must turn toward scripture under the pressure of this word *necessary*. Reading Moses and the prophets is transformed from an enquiry about what they said and meant, even what they may have foretold, to an enquiry into the deep mystery of necessity. And the search, already difficult and far from self-evident, happens under the press of Jesus' haunting question. As the angels' question ironically eclipsed the story-world of the women at the tomb, Jesus' question turns upon the reader in the same way.

How can one answer his question? Search back through the explicit interpretations of scripture in the Gospel and forward into Acts and there is no clear, unequivocal answer. To understand scripture is to understand how this suffering was necessary, yet that understanding is nowhere given or confirmed. One must read and think, but with the eyes focused above the page on a "virtual" scripture, a scripture "transfigured," as it were, by being seen in the light of Jesus' death and resurrection. For a guide there is only this imperative: to understand

and believe the scriptures, to understand and believe (in) Jesus, one must grasp what *suffering* means. To grasp who Jesus is— as the Human One, as prophet, Child of God, Messiah—one must grasp *his* particular suffering. That is to say, one must give his suffering a name.

There is at least one person in the Gospel who does this, who speaks directly of Jesus' suffering and puts a name to it. Upon Jesus' death, the centurion who witnessed the crucifixion praised God and said, "certainly this man was *dikaios.*" What *dikaios* means in this verse is open to some reflection. The more familiar reading is "innocent" (RSV), but there are other strong possibilities: "righteous" and "just."[5] While Jesus' innocence is undeniably the concern of the scenes before Pilate and the crowd, the theme of righteousness or justice, especially the kind associated with "the prophets," is even more deeply imprinted upon the narrative as a whole, beginning with Jesus' baptism and his interpretation of the scroll of Isaiah.[6] The Sermon on the Plain, Peter's confession, and the Transfiguration continue in the line, and include the link of prophecy and suffering.[7] Psalm 118, cited in both Luke (20:17) and Acts (4:11), emphasizes the dual themes of righteousness and suffering, and adds the dynamic, so important to Luke, of ironic reversal as well.

Out of my distress I called on the LORD . . .

All nations surrounded me . . .
I was pushed so hard, so that I was falling,
      but the LORD helped me.
The LORD is my strength and my might;
      and has become my salvation . . .

Open to me the gates of righteousness,
that I may enter through them
and give thanks to the LORD.

This is the gate of the LORD;
      the righteous shall enter through it.

I thank you that you have answered me
      and have become my salvation.
The stone that the builders rejected
      has become the chief cornerstone.
                    (Ps 118:5, 10, 13-14, 19-22)

Jesus is handed over, condemned, and crucified, not because he is innocent, but because he is righteous. In many ways the Jesus of Luke is not innocent at all. He offends religiously, socially, culturally, politically, and economically. He is numbered among the transgressors because he *is* a transgressor.[8] Jesus' death in Luke is the death of the transgressor who is just, and who dies because of the dispute over what justice is.[9] "Certainly," says the centurion, "this man was just."

It is this Jesus the Righteous One who is proclaimed by the apostles in their preaching in Acts. In Solomon's Portico, Peter declares him the "Holy and Righteous One," whom God raised up to bless the people by turning them "from their wicked ways" (3:14-26). Stephen enrages the council through his proclamation that it is Jesus who is the Righteous One foretold by the prophets, prophets who were killed for their prophecy; Jesus is the one who keeps the Law of God (7:52-53). Philip affirms to the Ethiopian that Jesus' death was the denial of justice (8:33-35). Paul declares to the Athenians the judgment of righteousness for which God appointed the Risen One (17:31). As Paul himself recounts his conversion, Ananais had told him how "The God of our ancestors has chosen you to know his will, to see the Righteous One and to hear his own voice" (22:14; cf. 9:17). In his defense before Felix, Paul asserts that he is really on trial because of his faith in the resurrection of the dead to judgment and justice (24:15-21). Before Agrippa he insists upon this again, and adds that the risen Jesus appointed him in order that he might testify to the people, so they would turn from the power of Satan to God, that is, to righteousness. Paul finally declares that it was for this very reason—that repentance and forgiveness be proclaimed—that Jesus suffered, died, and was raised (26:8, 17-18, 23). The Suffering One is the Righteous One. The Righteous One is the Risen One. The Risen One is the Judge who proclaims justice and calls upon the world to turn from the power of injustice.

In the preaching of the apostles in Acts, then, here is why it is necessary that the Messiah suffer and die. To do justice means to suffer, and great justice means great suffering. That is not the will of God but in the nature of justice itself and in the

128

way of the world. God raised Jesus from the dead to declare that in Jesus is indeed the righteousness of God. It is by Jesus that righteousness will be judged for the living and the dead, and Jesus invites all the world to repentance for the forgiveness of sins and a life of justice on the Way. "Was it not necessary?"

What, then, is the suffering of Jesus? Call it the suffering of the Just One. That, at least, is a starting point. One must still search far beyond these stories through the scriptures, with little more than a centurion's confession as a clue, and with no way finally to know if it is a false lead to begin with. One must ask after the visible and invisible suffering. Who suffers? How and why? What becomes of suffering? What does it tell about the future? What are the meanings of justice? What is God's justice? How does it all point with the force of necessity, a necessity which leads to a Messiah who is handed over, condemned, crucified, and risen? How can the word "salvation" be the outcome? Suffering, justice, and necessity, . . . there are so many different ways they might combine, so many different stories they might reinterpret. So many different songs and poems and oracles might greet each other and a reader in new ways! However that may be, in this story of the road to Emmaus the burden has shifted and the pressure has turned upon the reader. Answer, now. "Was it not necessary?"

WHOSE EYES ARE HELD? WHOSE ARE OPENED?

As they came near the village to which they were going, he walked ahead as if he were going on. But they urged him strongly, saying, "Stay with us, because it is almost evening and the day is now nearly over." So he went in to stay with them. When he was at the table with them, he took bread, blessed and broke it, and gave it to them. Then their eyes were opened, and they recognized him; and he vanished from their sight. They said to each other, "Were not our hearts burning within us while he was talking to us on the road, while he was opening the scriptures to us?"

The story is not about how the disciples themselves finally came to recognize the stranger as the risen Jesus, because the story is not *about* them. It is about when and how they were *allowed* to recognize Jesus, and what form that recognition took. From the beginning of the story, when it was told how the disciples were held from recognition, this has been the question. How and when will their eyes be released so they can recognize the Jesus they know? Much is shrouded. We do not know who held their eyes to begin with. Was it Jesus himself? Was it another "character" who never appears in the story, but who is the author of the deep necessity of all that has been written and done? The story does not say.

Now we must also ask about another necessity, the necessity of veiling their eyes. Why was it necessary that the disciples be prevented from recognizing Jesus until they had told their story, had the scriptures revealed to them, and witnessed the bread broken? Because there are no words from Jesus or the narrator to explain, we must be careful not to say too certainly what the text has so clearly kept uncertain or even hidden.

If there is to be an "explanation" one must begin by taking seriously the story itself. Because this is a plot-dominated story (whereas one might argue the Gospel as a whole to be character-dominated), it is especially helpful to consider the initiation of the plot, its rising action, and climax. This is done most easily by thinking backward from climax to beginning.

The disciples' eyes are released to recognize Jesus in the breaking of the bread. The bread was not broken until the disciples invited the wise stranger to stay with them. The wise stranger had mocked their foolishness and slow faith by interpreting to them how the scriptures showed the necessity of Jesus, the Just One, suffering and entering into glory. The interpretation was a correction of the disciples' own account of Jesus' work and death, and their response to it. That account was the result of being questioned by the apparently foolish stranger about their discussion of the events surrounding Jesus' death. The disciples' speech and actions only take the form they do because their eyes are prevented from recognizing the stranger as the risen Jesus. The scene is enacted in an indeterminate place on a road leading away from Jerusalem, and its characters are two disciples who are otherwise never mentioned.

The first thing to note about the role of the disciples' blindness is functional: all these events in the plot are held together by the veiling of the disciples' eyes. In a strictly literary sense, the author is faced with certain problems which the story creates and must solve. This is the first appearance of the risen Jesus for both the disciples and the reader. It is inevitable, therefore, that this will establish a pattern or model, and serve as the first interpretive key to the resurrection in the continuation of the story. What is included (and excluded), then, becomes highly significant; what is included must bear the weight of being the interpretive key to what follows.

The veiling of the disciples' eyes functions in several other ways. First, it establishes that the disciples are not the active agents in what follows; their role is essentially passive. This enhances the effect of indeterminacy which the setting of the story and its weak characterization achieve. If what follows is a paradigm, then, it is one established by Jesus, not by the disciples. Within the story, it is a divine pattern, not a human one.

Second, by setting up the veiled eyes as the problem, the author shows the reader how to recognize when the framing is complete. What is essential will happen within the frame of veiled eyes/open eyes.

Third, as long as the disciples' eyes remain veiled, the plot may not be prematurely concluded. This means that one particular moment in the plot is not privileged over what precedes or follows. Each step in the plot is a step toward the climax, and the climax needs each step.

Finally, with the completion of the frame by opening the disciples' eyes, the author signals that the set *within* the frame is complete, too. The frame is established for the sake of what happens within it. The disciples' eyes are released to "see" and recognize Jesus; the reader is released to "see" the story as a whole. When Jesus vanishes at the moment of recognition, the closing of the frame and the importance of what lies within it is emphasized even more. There are no further words or actions in the story to distract from the central plot, no details about the risen Jesus to draw attention away from the focal drama.

As a literary device, then, the veiling of the disciples' eyes works to hold together and order thematic elements which the author judges *need* to be held together and ordered in a story placed in such a position. Within this frame the author has placed an incomplete account, and a "wrong" interpretation, a verdict upon the mistaken interpreters, an affirmation of the positive relationship between Jesus' suffering and the scriptures, a narrative statement about the stranger/Jesus interpreting for the disciples what the scriptures say about him, an invitation, a meal, and ritual actions by the stranger/Jesus on the same pattern as the Last Supper and the Feeding of the Multitude (22:19ff, 9:10ff). On the literary level, these are meant to be read together as culminating in the release of the disciples' eyes and their recognition of Jesus. The story is structured in such a way that the recognition of Jesus depends upon all these things together. Recognition will not happen until all of them are in place and in order. In all of this the disciples are not the focus because they are not the active agents; Jesus is the one who makes the pattern, and the pattern is of his own action.

The frame device of holding/opening functions literarily, certainly; but it is more than "just" a literay device. It has a content of its own. By using this opposition for the paradigmatic resurrection appearance story, the author identifies what "problem" is being worked on—what the chief question about the resurrection is for the larger story at hand. As we have noted, the frame exists for the sake of what is within it, but the reverse is true as well. Only if the problem is great enough does it have the power to hold things together; only if the outcome is sufficiently important (either in the world of the story itself or for the reader), can it sustain the suspense and delay necessary to bring all the elements together. The problem which the author chooses has to do less with resurrection than with presence. It has to do with recognizing presence in the scriptures, in events, and in experience. It could be stated this way: why does the risen Jesus come near but make one unable to recognize who he is? What is the experience of Jesus' presence?

In this story of the appearance of the risen Jesus, the experience of his presence takes the form of *recognition*. Recognition is depicted as seeing truly the identity of the Jesus who had been with them all along. Recognition is the experience of an instant which changes perception. Within the story it is an experience of revelation, in a particular sense.[10] The revelation is not of a knowledge or meaning, as in the stranger's teaching of the scripture; rather it is a revelation of presence. The moment of recognition (the moment of realized presence), however, ends as soon as the disciples become aware of it. Jesus is revealed as *having been* present, and the fleeting experience of recognition turns immediately toward memory. The disciples now recognize the Jesus who had been present to them without their knowledge, and whose presence changes the story of the past. The transformation of the present moment by recognition takes the form of a transformation of the story of the past. Memory is converted by presence, and is retold as the story of the hidden presence of the suffering Jesus who did not allow himself to be recognized.

In the logic of this story-world, then, Jesus is the Just One, who therefore suffers death because of the nature of his justice and the nature of the world. The scriptures reveal the deep necessity of both of these. Suffering is transformed into glory through resurrection, thereby confirming that this was God's justice and revealing a new story about the way of justice. As the Just One, Jesus rises from death and returns to the community of followers to teach them his true story—a story which the disciples will continue to read as a promise about the future in a story about the past. The followers, however, will experience that presence in a momentary recognition which has no content of itself. It is simply a moment of presence, the effect of which is that the disciples then discover the presence of the hidden Jesus in their own re-remembered story.

What now has become of the plot in which the reader is a character? Has that plot reached a climax as well? At the beginning of the story, the disciples' eyes were held, while the reader knew everything. With the disciples' telling of the story, the reader remains on the inside, but something has started to change. The narrative places their account in the wrong but does not say *how* it is in the wrong. One knows *why* it must be wrong: it does not include the resurrection, which changes everything. To say *how* that changes the story, however, one must tell it correctly, that is, differently.

Who will do such a telling? Has the reader's inside position given that ability? Knowing the resurrection, could the reader yet tell the story of Jesus, the mighty words and deeds, in such a way that the true end is discernable within them, and more than discernable, even necessary (as the angels had said it was)? Is even this Gospel adequate to the need? If it were, then the reader should be able to give the true account, including the necessity of "handed over, condemned, crucified." By displaying the inadequate account in this way (that is, through actually recounting it in dialogue, instead of simply referring to it through narration), the question and anticipation of the true account is sharpened. An expectation of symmetry suggests that in what follows the true account will be given, thereby maintaining the reader as insider. Instead of that account, however, we find only an ironic statement *about* the true account, an account which is hidden in narration.

In this way there is a dis-ease introduced into the reader's position. Still it is inside, but it begins to become evident that it is inside only to a certain extent, and only because the narrator, or another, has chosen to place one there for reasons which are not given. What one sees or does not see—whether one's eyes are held shut or opened—is determined by a power which is unnamed. There is the voice of the narrator, but there is another presence also. The presence has no voice; instead it has power to give and withhold, to open and close. In the story itself there is a presence whose name is not mentioned, who is "author" of this resurrection from the dead. In the *text* there is also such a presence at work.[11] The narrator speaks to the reader just as the stranger speaks to the disciples. The reader's eyes are veiled just as the disciples' are, yet because of the "inside" position, the veiling is not yet apparent. With the opening of the disciples' eyes, the reader's position is revealed as well. The reader has not really been seeing from the inside, but this fiction has been as necessary as the fiction of a stranger walking along the road.

Why the necessity of veiling the reader's eyes? It works the reversal of the reader—from one who knows to one who must be taught; from one who tells a story the way an author does to one who enacts a story authored by another; from one who grasps the shape of the world to one whose world is eclipsed. The reader witnesses the surprising and reversing of the disciples, unaware that it is the reader's own reversal which is being prepared.

The reversal which can be discerned at the level of reading is also more than a "device," just as it was in the story of the disciples. It has a theological force and content as well. The story has been given, but not the "story of the story." This story being read points away from itself to a meta-story of deep necessity which is unwritten and untold. That story is in, under, around, and through, all other stories, which are to this deep story as the letter is to the book. The answer has not been given, but withheld. Because it is withheld, the reader is forced onto the road of interpretation where nothing is self-evident— not memory, not scripture, not Jesus, not hope. One only approaches this deep story through talking of "all these things" together, telling what you can (inevitably wrongly), listening for the voices of strangers who turn your world upside down, and, in the briefest moments of recognition, realizing who the companions have been. And as a guide for such travellers to steer by there are these three stars: necessity, suffering, justice.

In the conclusion of Luke's Gospel and the beginning of Acts, Jesus is lifted up to heaven. The mighty words and deeds have been accomplished, and the teaching about the realm of God by the Risen Messiah has been given. No more will Jesus' presence to the community be known directly. It will be, instead, the presence of the Holy Spirit, recognized in the empowerment of the followers to witness to the Righteous One, that is, to tell the story. Henceforth Jesus as Jesus will be absent.[12] To know Jesus will now mean to know Jesus' story, to know it as the Just One's story, flowing deep beneath the surface of the scriptures, deep in memory, deep within the struggle of the faithful community. Jesus will be known in interpretation.

THE EXEGESIS OF PRESENCE

The story of the Road to Emmaus, as we have followed it, presents the dynamic of interpretation as a narrative dynamic. The picture of interpretation which emerges is fixed upon a field of story, as the photographic image is fixed upon a field of paper. Interpretation here is the bringing together of events and words into the particular coherence of a story, not a system. In particular it means to build a story of the future, a story of hope, through the telling of the story of the past. To do so means that the interpreter must face the question of what sort of "text" tells the story of the past and points to the future with the character of promise. Within the Emmaus story in particular, and Luke-Acts in general, we have proposed that the true story of the past is the one epitomized in Jesus, because it is revealed in the resurrection to be the story God authors. The text of that past is not to be read as one of words and deeds, mighty and powerful, which promise a future of the same; rather, it is to be read as the text of righteousness or justice, suffering because of the nature of justice itself, and redeemed by God in the resurrection of Jesus. For the followers, to be redeemed in the present means to be freed from the past by forgiveness, which is itself a transformation of the memory of the past, the story of the past. It also means to be given Spirit to re-tell the story of the Just One, and to enact that story in the present as a promise and a call to righteousness.

The present is the time of interpretation. It is the time when memory is transformed into the story of the presence of the Just One who suffered; and the time when scripture is transformed into the story of that story's necessity. Interpretation, whether of scripture, experience, or memory, becomes the search for the story of suffering justice. This suffering, wherever it is found, is part of the story of Jesus, and interpretation tells it in such a way that this suffering reaches its fullest expression and deepest clarity in "handed over, condemned, crucified, and risen." Interpretation tells a story of the future which is a story of suffering justice redeemed and transformed. The realm of God is the realm of suffering justice redeemed. To tell a story about the future, then, the interpreter turns to the texts of suffering justice and tells them as a promise of the transformation and redemption witnessed in the resurrection of Jesus. The face of glory can only be recognized in the face of suffering justice transformed by the presence of the Just One. Within this story-world, then, interpretation becomes an exegesis of presence whereby the Just One becomes present in transformed stories of memory and hope.

We began with photographs of people reading and questions about the mystery captured in those images. Having dwelt some little while on the Road to Emmaus, it is time to return to the pictures. Each one is a fragment of a story, as we have noted. Each is the fragment of a particular story which stretches forward and back from the crystallized moment. It is the power of a photograph, however, to bestow a gravity upon the instant, to grant it the power of emblems or holy objects. Within its frame the photograph is a sanctuary for time; within it is not something timeless, but time grown ripe and held in a perfection that is foreign to experience, allowing one to dwell upon the mystery to which each moment opens. Or to return to the word "sacrament," one could call a photograph a sacrament of time. Of itself it is only a piece of paper patterned by shadows—an absence. But by the peculiar faith we call imagination, the viewer may feast upon presence.

The story of the road to Emmaus presses upon the interpreter to read the scriptures and experience in precisely the same way. It makes reading into a search for presence which may fix its eye upon a photograph in a book as hopefully and expectantly as upon a page of Moses and all the prophets. For that search, these photographs of reading have a particular gift to give. In each one the gift is different, and in each one it is the same. Each is a particular story—ripe, as every story is, with the question of justice and suffering redeemed; and so each one brings a particular human face to the facelessness of the search. With light and shadow for body and blood, a face, a place, a time, a page, an imaged instant is offered for recognition. This is the place of the search. These are the conditions. Here is where presence must be met if anywhere at all. And each one is ripe with *the* story, the story of the Human One, the Child of

God, Holy and Righteous, the Messiah who went about doing good and freeing those who were oppressed by the devil, the Just One who was handed over, condemned, crucified. Each one is ripe with the story of the stranger who tells stories of the deep mystery of justice, and who vanishes into the page and into the reckoned moments of experience, there to be sought and found in the story of resurrection given in words and deeds that tell the truth of the suffering, and the truth of the joy. This is the exegesis of presence.

7

THE
PASSION
OF
INTERPRETATION

STORIES, NOT SYSTEMS

Interpretation is in crisis, which is a good thing. The crisis has come as foundations of perception, thinking, experience, and community have been challenged and re-examined, not only by scholars but by many others as well. Kierkegaard observed in one of his journal entries that every human life ought to have "primitivity." By that odd word he meant the re-examination of the foundations of experience and existence. The genius of such "primitivity," he insisted, is not to produce something new, but to ask about fundamental questions from the particularity of a life, place, and time (in Hong & Hong 1967:no. 657). When such a re-examination happens, he recognized, systems are shaken. An honesty, an authenticity, becomes possible which possesses a far greater coherence than an intellectual system ever could. But it is a coherence of a different kind. Call it the coherence by which thinking and living express one another: one actually lives in the categories of one's thought; one thinks in the actual categories of one's life.

In some ways that would seem to be the essence of simplicity, and that is, indeed, what Kierkegaard called it (see nos. 663, 665). Simplicity or honesty, however, is never simple to achieve; it may be what is hardest of all. Perhaps that is why we struggle so intensely with questions of race, gender, class, culture, sexual orientation, person, experience, mind. It is simply so difficult to see, speak, and act in this kind of honesty. The task requires, paradoxically, such great power of concentration *and* great power of letting go. A single lived honesty is so costly it must be held fast, but it can only be held fast honestly if it is released again and again to relearn its truth.

What we have done here is to suggest an approach to thinking about interpretation in such a time of holding fast and letting go. It is an approach which seeks to honor both the new life from which the crisis has emerged and the perpetual need to make sense (however provisionally) even when so much is uncertain. We have tried to think about the nature of interpretation through thinking within the dynamics of narrative. This approach is founded upon the recent reassessment of narrative as foundational to human experience, thinking, and acting. The focus, however, has not been on narrative or experience *as such*. These are both abstractions, beasts we shall never see. To work with narrative, of course, requires narratives—stories which in their concreteness and particularity are counterparts in form to the stories of concrete and particular human experience.

The initial approach, the starting place, has been an understanding of the nature of interpretation based primarily upon the work of Paul Ricoeur, in terms of both the arc of interpretation as a whole, and the dialectic of explanation and understanding. It has been a dual approach of exegesis and hermeneutics, or in literary terms, of both criticism and poetics. We have attempted through an exegesis to grasp meaning in a text, and then have turned such meaning back upon the question of interpretation, asking what these stories teach us about how we make sense, how we read the signs, events, and texts of our world into a world, and how we might represent that work to ourselves. It is a reflection upon the person of the interpreter who, to borrow Foucault's language (1973:352), "from within the life to which he [sic] entirely belongs and by which he is traversed in his whole being, constitutes representations by means of which he lives, and on the basis of which he possesses that strange capacity of being able to represent to himself precisely that life."

Interpretation, we have posited, is founded upon a story about meaning, a story set—as any story must be—within a world of characters, possibilities, relationships, needs, and difficulties. In the story of Hermes it was a tale of desire seeking what it believed to be its own, enacting a fiction, performing a fantastic theater of desire at the boundaries of such things as past and present, fixed and open, inclusion and exclusion, lie and truth, wild and tame, belief and unbelief.

In the story of Eliezar and the Sages it was a tale of meaning and authority, scripture and interpreter, individual and community, heaven and earth all in collision, judged by the testimony of tears.

In the story of the Binding of Isaac it was a story about the refusal and resistance of meaning, and how that led to a search beyond the story itself through the deep echoes of language, imagination, and memory.

In the stories of Isak Dinesen, interpretation became a search to read what had not been written, a search for the Other in the scandal of difference and identity, enacted through a loyalty of presence, a loyalty to the life which blood inscribes.

Finally, in the story of the Road to Emmaus, interpretation became the search for the hidden presence of the Just One in the pages of the scripture and in the experience of the community, in the mystery and necessity of justice suffering and suffering redeemed.

These are the barest sketches of the stories, of course, and no story can be reduced to its plot and remain itself—certainly not these. There always remains a powerful residue of image and metaphor, of questions and possibilities which defy categorization or systemization. Stanley Hauerwas and David Burrell (1989), in considering the role of narratives in forming our ideas of what we should do and who we should be, insist that the complexity and richness of our inherited moral thought is founded upon the profusion and contrariness of the stories we know and tell. What is needed, they conclude, is to develop the ability to understand such stories and how they work in us.

> It is not theory-building that develops such a capacity so much as close attention to the ways our distinctive communities tell their stories. . . . The legitimate human concern for rationality is framed by a range of power of quite another order. It is this larger contingent context which narrative is designed to order in the only manner available to us. (1989:170, 176)

Our interpretive thought is heir to the same rich and contrary profusion of stories. To gather certain stories together as we have here, then, is not to make a single theory which binds them together, but to undertake this task of reflection upon how such stories work, and how they illuminate other stories which are also at work. In place of the coherence of a system, then, one has a different coherence, that of a "canon" of stories. Doubtless there is also a canon-within-the-canon, a group of stories which for an individual or community centers and orients the others. And doubtless there is a canon-beyond-the-canon, a group of stories which may be unacknowledged but are powerfully at work in shaping the understanding of the acknowledged ones. To explore such stories is not to weave them into a seamless garment, but to follow them into the fundamentals of interpretation. Who knows? Perhaps one of them might lead to the sort of astonishment by which the unthinkable becomes thinkable, the invisible becomes visible, the unheard of heard.

PASSION

In the stories we have encountered here, interpretation is a work of passion. It begins in passion, proceeds through passion, and finally arrives in passion. Passion is a word of many senses. Passion has to do with love, hate, desire, and hunger. Passion is intensity and determination. Passion is power and the source of power. Passion is vocation and calling. Passion is giving oneself over to something outside oneself. Passion is the object toward which one's life is turned. For the Christian church, of course, the word has a special sense. Passion is the suffering of Christ, in the garden and on the cross. It is the suffering, also, of those in whom our imaginations see it all—not again—but for the first time. To speak of passion in this sense is to speak of the cost of love.

142

To say that interpretation is a work of passion includes all these senses. It is to emphasize how inevitably and properly personal this work is. Interpretation is grounded in memory and pain and joy, in the strongest love and most terrible fear, in nightmare and daydream and solitary vision that is too beautiful to be untrue, in the secret wells of power from which strength comes day after day.

To speak of passion is to emphasize how intimately interpretation is tied to persons, places, events, and times—persons one can name, places one can walk to, events one must rise to on a day which will never be repeated.

To speak of passion is to emphasize that the work is turned toward a horizon beyond—some community, some commitment, some justice, some vision, some future—which is known chiefly through the emblems and signs by which it pulls upon one's hope. It may be utterly individual or utterly global or utterly metaphysical, but that passion will reach into every step of the interpretive journey, and will shape it as surely as the moon pulls the tides.

To speak of passion is to speak finally of the work of interpretation as suffering the cost of love, bearing in one's body and spirit the cost of love, being changed by the cost of love, changed by love, changed for love, changed to love.

The passion of interpretation, I believe, will always have a story, and that story is the one in which, or for which, interpreters live and move and have their being. It will likely be a story impossible to tell because it is the one enacted day after day down the whole pilgrimage of a life. The stories we *can* tell are never *the* story. Call them places of hospitality on the road where one rests a while before moving on. Call them sanctuaries where we can gather for a while to meet the meanings of our lives in the solemn ceremony of time. Call them the wings of God, in the shelter of which a sojourner can sing for joy.

NOTES

BIBLIOGRAPHY

INDEXES

NOTES

NOTES TO CHAPTER 1:
STORIES OF INTERPRETATION

[1] This is the line of argument in Stephen Crites's often quoted "The Narrative Quality of Experience" (1971).

[2] See Jonathan Culler (1982:64-83). Culler uses the theme of "stories of reading" to describe a range of post-structuralist approaches to the problem of reading. The idea is shifted somewhat here and rendered more literal and "storylike," but my chief debt is to is Culler.

[3] Descriptions of the various elements of narrative vary somewhat, as do assessments of which elements are most important. I prefer a more flexible analytical model such as Wesley Kort's (1989), which grants the possibility of primacy to any of the elements in a given narrative, over one which insists upon character or plot, for example, as the determining element in every narrative.

NOTES TO CHAPTER 2:
THE EXEGESIS OF DESIRE

[1] This list is comprised of images of Hermes drawn from the "Hymn to Hermes," attributed to Homer, which is discussed below. It is not part of the work itself.

[2] The different approaches to myth surveyed here are based upon Lauri Honko (1984).

[3] This is the "detour" of Ricoeur's *Symbolism of Evil* (1967).

[4] The chief parallel to the story as a whole is found in *The Library*, conventionally attributed to Apollodorus, a grammarian of the second century BCE. The work is a sort of handbook of mythology, dating, in fact, from perhaps the first century CE. The version of the story Apollodorus tells is focused somewhat differently, and the difference helps distinguish the particular shading of the "Hymn."

In part, the difference results from an alternative approach to composition. While the "Hymn" attends carefully to dialogue, movement, and emotion, Apollodorus' account is purely external narration. It recounts actions and outcomes, not speech and motives. In this version of the story, lacking speech, Hermes is primarily a thief, not a liar or a person who manipulates words, and certainly not one who interprets the desire that governs his actions. In Apollodorus' version the scandal and opposition are softened and diffused. The cleverness and cunning of the thief stands in no particular opposition to the function of the herald; stealth and secrecy may in fact be useful for carrying out certain commissions. By comparison it becomes apparent that theft is overshadowed and eclipsed by desire for place, deception, lying, and false swearing. By comparison, the granting of the herald's staff is thrown into sharpest relief by the relationship of Hermes to speech. For Hermes speech is supremely fluid, volatile, and plastic. It always has a double referent: one which seems to be, and one which is hidden—often the exact opposite of what seems to be.

[5] For a general discussion of Apollo see H. J. Rose (1928:134f).

[6] For the philological material see Liddell and Scott (1940); see also Kittel (1965) on *keryx*.

[7] See Brown (1947:33). Brown's analysis deals with Hermes as a psycho-social type emblematic of the rising class of artisans and merchants, and depicts the struggle with Apollo as a social struggle for power with the aristocracy.

[8] See Robert Graves (1960:I.56.e).

[9] Burkert (1985:158). For a somewhat Jungian treatment of Hermes as the guide to souls, see Karl Kerenyi (1976).

[10] (1973; D. Wender, trans.).

[11] On the relationship of fiction to history or "true stories," see Paul Ricoeur (1981).

[12] This will be recognized as a kind of structuralist actantial model along the lines of A. J. Greimas. See Culler (1977), or Daniel Patte (1976).

NOTES TO CHAPTER 3:
THE EXEGESIS OF TEARS

[1] All citations from the Talmud are taken from the translation by H. Freedman (1959).

[2] An excellent and accessible introduction to the history of biblical interpretation beginning with Jesus is Robert M. Grant and David Tracy (1984).

[3] See Renee Bloch (1978:29-50).

[4] This discussion of midrash is a combined account based upon Bloch, Neusner, Handelman, and Bruns above, and Michael Fishbane (1985; 1986). See also David Stern (1984) and James Kugel (1984).

[5] This is in Bruns' version of the story. His perspective and language often show strong affinity with Hans-Georg Gadamer and Paul Ricoeur. Others with different philosophical lenses (e.g., Handelman) will cast rabbinic interpretation according to their own particular philosophical commitments. As in everything, what is seen depends upon who looks.

[6] My thanks to Professor Andre LaCocque for his verdict upon the verse.

[7] An extended example of communal Christian "midrash" may be found in Ernesto Cardenal (1976).

NOTES TO CHAPTER 4:
THE EXEGESIS OF ECHOES

[1] For a range of essays concerning reader-response criticism, see Jane P. Tompkins (1980).

[2] A key difference, perhaps, is that for Levertov the literary author would seem to be the author of our reading experience, while certain reader-response critics would push for a more radically reader-centered understanding of where authorship of the reading experience lies. The horizon, however, is broad enough to include both possibilities.

[3] Erich Auerbach's celebrated study (1965) describes the story as "fraught with background."

[4] For a commentary upon Rabbinic interpretations of the "Akeda," see Elie Wiesel (1976:83-116).

[5] See Wiesel (1976:105-107).

[6] Bobbie Groth, 1989, unpublished manuscript.

NOTES TO CHAPTER 5:
THE EXEGESIS OF THE UNWRITTEN

[1] See Susan Gubar (1982). Susan Hardy Aiken (1990) recently related Dinesen to feminist psychoanalytical theories and post-structuralist thought, including French writers Cixous, Irigaray, and Kristeva.

[2] See, for example, Susan Brooks Thistlethwaite (1989), a white American feminist who considers certain connections of race, gender, and religion through dialogue with African-American women and their literature.

[3] Seymour Chatman (1978:26f). Chatman draws upon Roman Ingarden's distinction between the "real object" and the "aesthetic object," combined with Susanne Langer's "virtual object," to discuss

the relationship between the narrative which is written, acted, filmed, painted, told, sung, etc. (the real object), and the one which is constructed or reconstructed in the observer's mind (the aesthetic or virtual object). The idea here is similar, but Dinesen's use of the word "loyalty" suggests a particular kind of relationship which the more distanced philosophical use does not. See also Langer (1953).

[4] See Chatman and Langer in note 3 above.

[5] The term "carnival" is drawn from Mikhail Bakhtin (esp. 1984) and his analysis of the social and literary function of carnival in medieval France. See also the exploration and expansion of his ideas in Stallybrass and White (1986). For a feminist consideration of both, see Clair Wills (1989:130-52).

[6] The understanding of metaphor is drawn from Paul Ricoeur. See in particular "Metaphor and the Main Problem of Hermeneutics" (1978). For the discussion of the characteristics of living and dead metaphor see *The Rule of Metaphor* (1978). The same discussion is applied to the question of dialogue here.

[7] See Susanne K. Langer (1953:306ff).

[8] I have in mind here the idea of the "virtual" object of a narrative, a term used by Langer (see notes 3, 4, and 7, above). The narrative reconstructed or actualized in the reader is the real reference of the story. The term "world" is a possible substitution; see Langer (1953:260-65).

NOTES TO CHAPTER 6:
THE EXEGESIS OF PRESENCE

[1] See Luke 3:22; 4:24; 7:37; 13:33; Acts 2:22; and 10:38. For a literary reading of Luke-Acts which explores the narrative unity of the texts, see Robert Tannehill (1986).

[2] "Human One" is the translation preferred by the *Inclusive Language Lectionary* (1983).

[3] There is a pattern of ironic reversal throughout Luke-Acts which plays on the theme of human misperception and recognition. See Tannehill (1986:283ff).

[4] Walter Ong (1982) contrasts the way in which primary oral cultures reshape "memory" in order to reflect the present situation with the way writing privileges the past.

[5] See Robert J. Karris (1986:65-74). The argument builds upon the insight that Luke is an independent theologian who writes from a different vision of Jesus' death than the sacrifice-atonement theme.

"God graciously vindicates . . . Jesus and creates salvific trust in those who trust in his justice" (74).

[6] See Luke 23:41, 50; Acts 3:14-15; 7:52; 22:14. On the relationship between the crucifixion and Acts, see Richard J. Dillon (1978:100-101).

[7] For a discussion of the pattern of prophetic suffering depicted in Luke, and its application to the necessity of Jesus' death, see Tannehill (1986:287-88). There it is understood as a pattern of prophetic destiny which connects Jesus with the prophets who came before and the followers who come after.

[8] For a discussion of the charges against Jesus and their aptness within the Lukan narrative, see Daryl Schmit (1983). The particular question of Luke's presentation of the conflict between rich and poor and Jesus' position in it is explored in Robert J. Karris (1978). A much more extensive treatment is found in Halvor Moxnes (1988).

[9] Jesus' death in Luke is not an atoning, substitutionary death. The question of whether it is a martyr's death is debated. Pro, see Charles Talbert (1983:99-110); con, see Karris (1978:68ff).

[10] Diana Culbertson (1989) identifies recognition as the beginning of religious experience, and examines recognition in certain classics of Western Literature as well as in the gospels of Mark and John.

[11] Meir Sternberg's study (1985) demonstrates ways in which certain narrative strategies in the Hebrew Bible correspond to the theological concern for God's omnipotence. The enquiry here moves in a similar direction by asking about the correlation between God/ Jesus/disciples and author/narrator/reader.

[12] "More consistently than any other New Testament writing, Acts presents Jesus as exalted and, as it were, temporarily 'absent,' but 'represented' on earth in the meantime by the Spirit" (C. F. D. Moule 1980:179).

BIBLIOGRAPHY

Aiken, Susan Hardy. 1990. *Isak Dinesen and the Engendering of Narrative*. Chicago: Univ. of Chicago.

Allen, Thomas W. and E. E. Sikes. 1904. *The Homeric Hymns*. London: Macmillan.

Auerbach, Erich. 1965. *Mimesis*. Princeton: Princeton Univ.

Augustine. 1950. *The City of God*. M. Dodds, trans. New York: Modern Library.

Bakhtin, Mikhail. 1984. *Rabelais and His World*. H. Iswolsky, trans. Bloomington: Indiana Univ.

Bloch, Renee. 1978. "Midrash." In *Approaches to Ancient Judaism*. W. S. Green, ed. Missoula: Scholars.

Brown, Norman O. 1947. *Hermes the Thief*. Madison: Univ. of Wisconsin.

Brueggemann, Walter. 1982. *Genesis*. Interpretation. Atlanta: John Knox.

Bruns, Gerald. 1987. "Midrash and Allegory." In *The Literary Guide to the Bible*. R. Alter and F. Kermode, eds. Cambridge: Harvard Univ.

Burkert, Walter. 1985. *Greek Religions*. Cambridge: Harvard Univ.

Cardenal, Ernesto. 1976. *The Gospel in Solentiname*. 4 vols. Maryknoll, NY: Orbis Books.

Chartier, Émile. 1973. *The Gods*. R. Peavar, trans. New York: New Directions.

Chatman, Seymour. 1978. *Story and Discourse: Narrative Structure in Fiction and Film*. Ithaca: Cornell Univ.

Creeley, Robert. 1982. "Poems Are a Complex." In *Claims for Poetry*. D. Hall, ed. Ann Arbor: Univ. of Michigan.

Crites, Stephen. 1971. "The Narrative Quality of Experience." *Journal of the American Academy of Religion* 39:291-311.

———. 1975. "Angels We Have Heard." In *Religion as Story*. J. B. Wiggins, ed. New York: Harper & Row.

Culbertson, Diana. 1989. *The Poetics of Revelation: Recognition and the Narrative Tradition*. Studies in American Biblical Hermeneutics 4. Macon: Mercer Univ.

Culler, Jonathan. 1982. *On Deconstruction: Theory and Criticism After Structuralism*. Ithaca: Cornell Univ.

Dillon, Richard J. 1978. *From Eye-Witnesses to Ministers of the Word:*

Tradition and Composition in Luke 24. Rome: Biblical Institute.

Dinesen, Isak. 1975. *Last Tales*. New York: Vintage.

Doniger O'Flaherty, Wendy. 1988. *Other Peoples' Myths*. New York: Macmillan.

Eliach, Yaffa. 1982. *Hasidic Tales of the Holocaust*. New York: Avon.

Fishbane, Michael. 1985. *Biblical Interpretation in Ancient Israel*. Oxford: Clarendon.

———. 1986. "Inner Biblical Exegesis: Types and Strategies of Interpretation in Ancient Israel." In *Midrash and Literature*. G. H. Hartman and S. Budick, eds. New Haven and London: Yale Univ.

Foucault, Michel. 1973. *The Order of Things*. New York: Random House and Vintage.

Freedman, H., trans. 1959. *The Babylonian Talmud*. Rebecca Bennet Publications.

Grant, Robert M. and David Tracy. 1984. *A Short History of the Interpretation of the Bible*. Philadelphia: Fortress.

Graves, Robert. 1960. *The Greek Myths*. New York: Viking.

Gubar, Susan. 1982. "'The Blank Page' and Female Creativity." In *Writing and Sexual Difference*. E. Abel, ed. Chicago: Univ. of Chicago.

Handelman, Susan. 1982. *The Slayers of Moses*. Albany: SUNY.

Hauerwas, Stanley and David Burrell. 1989. "From System to Story: An Alternative Pattern for Rationality in Ethics." In *Why Narrative: Readings in Narrative Theology*. S. Hauerwas and L. Gregory Jones, eds. Grand Rapids: Eerdmans.

Hawkes, Terence. 1977. *Structuralism and Semiotics*. Berkeley: Univ. of California.

Hesiod and Theogonis. 1973. D. Wender, trans. New York: Penguin.

Honko, Lauri. 1984. "The Problem of Defining Myth." In *Sacred Narrative: Readings in the Theory of Myth*. A. Dundes, ed. Berkeley: Univ. of California.

Inclusive Language Lectionary. 1983. National Council of Churches, The Cooperative Publication Association.

Iser, Wolfgang. 1980. "The Reading Process: A Phenomenological Approach." In *Reader-response Criticism: From Formalism to Post-Structuralism*. J. P. Tompkins, ed. Baltimore: Johns Hopkins.

Jabès, Edmond. 1972. *The Book of Questions*. R. Waldrop, trans. Middletown: Wesleyan.

Karris, Robert J. 1978. "The Lukan *Sitz im Leben*." In *Perspectives on Luke-Acts*. C. Talbert, ed. Perspectives In Religious Studies, Special Studies Series 5. Danville, VA: Association of Baptist Professors of Religion.

———. 1986. "Luke 23:47 and the Lukan View of Jesus' Death." *Journal of Biblical Literature* 105:65-74.

Kerenyi, Karl. 1976. *Hermes: Guide of Souls*. Dallas: Spring.

Kierkegaard, Soren. 1941. *Concluding Unscientific Postscript*. D. F. Swenson and W. Lowrie, trans. Princeton: Princeton Univ.

——. 1954. *Fear and Trembling and Sickness Unto Death*. W. Lowrie, trans. Princeton: Princeton Univ.

——. 1967. *Soren Kierkegaard's Journals and Papers*. H. V. Hong and E. H. Hong, eds. and trans. Bloomington and London: Indiana Univ.

Kirk, G. S. 1984. "On Defining Myth." In *Sacred Narrative*. A. Dundes, ed. Berkeley: Univ. of California.

Kittel, Gerhard, ed. 1965. *Theological Dictionary of the New Testament*. Grand Rapids: Eerdmans.

Kort, Wesley A. 1989. *Story, Text, and Scripture*. Univ. Park: Pennsylvania State Univ.

Kugel, James. 1984. "Two Introductions to Midrash." *Prooftexts* 4.

Langbaum, Robert. 1975. *Isak Dinesen's Art: The Gayety of Vision*. Chicago: Univ. of Chicago.

Langer, Susanne K. 1953. *Feeling and Form*. New York: Scribners.

Levertov, Denise. 1982. "On the Function of the Line." In *Claims for Poetry*. D. Hall, ed. Ann Arbor: Univ. of Michigan.

Liddell and Scott. 1940. *A Greek-English Lexicon*. Oxford: Clarendon.

Luther, Martin. 1964. *Lectures on Genesis: Chapters 21-25*. J. Pelikan, ed. St. Louis: Concordia.

Moule, C. F. D. 1980. "The Christology of Acts." In *Studies in Luke-Acts*. L. Keck and J. L. Martyn, eds. Philadelphia: Fortress.

Moxnes, Halvor. 1988. *The Economy of the Kingdom: Social Conflict and Economic Relations in Luke's Gospel*. Philadelphia: Fortress.

Neusner, Jacob. 1987. *What is Midrash?*. Philadelphia: Fortress.

Ong, Walter. 1982. *Orality and Literacy: The Technologizing of the Word*. London and New York: Methuen.

Ovid. 1955. *The Metamorphoses of Ovid*. M. M. Innes, trans. New York: Penguin.

Owen, Wilfred. 1986. *The Poems of Wilfred Owen*. J. Stallworthy, ed. New York and London: W. W. Norton.

Patte, Daniel. 1976. *What Is Structural Exegesis?* Philadelphia: Fortress.

Ricoeur, Paul. 1978. "Metaphor and the Main Problem of Hermeneutics." In *The Philosophy of Paul Ricoeur*. C. E. Reagen and D. Stewart, eds. Boston: Beacon.

——. 1967. *The Symbolism of Evil*. E. Buchanan, trans. New York: Harper & Row.

——. 1981. "The Narrative Function." In *Hermeneutics & The Human Sciences*. J. B. Thompson, ed. and trans. Cambridge: Cambridge Univ.

——. 1978. *The Rule of Metaphor*. R. Czerny, trans. London: Routledge and Kegan Paul.

Rose, H. J. 1928. *A Handbook of Greek Mythology*. London: Methuen.

Schmit, Daryl. 1983. "Luke's 'Innocent' Jesus: A Scriptural Apologetic." In *Political Issues in Luke-Acts*. R. J. Cassidy and P. J. Scharper, eds. Maryknoll: Orbis.

Stallybrass, Peter and Allon White. 1986. *The Politics and Poetics of Transgression*. Ithaca: Cornell Univ.

Stern, David. 1984. "Midrash and the Language of Exegesis." *Prooftexts* 4.

Sternberg, Meir. 1985. *The Poetics of Biblical Narrative: Ideological Literature and the Drama of Reading*. Bloomington: Indiana Univ.

Talbert, Charles. 1983. "Martyrdom in Luke-Acts and the Lukan Social Ethic." In *Political Issues in Luke-Acts*. R. J. Cassidy and P. J. Scharper, eds. Maryknoll: Orbis.

Tannehill, Robert. 1986. *The Narrative Unity of Luke-Acts*. Philadelphia: Fortress.

The Odyssey. 1961. R. Fitzgerald, trans. Garden City: Anchor.

The Iliad. 1975. R. Fitzgerald, trans. Garden City: Anchor.

The Homeric Hymns. 1976. A. N. Athanassakis, trans. Baltimore: Johns Hopkins.

Thistlethwaite, Susan Brooks. 1989. *Sex, Race, and God*. New York: Crossroads.

Todorov, Tzvetan. 1973. *The Fantastic: A Structural Approach to A Literary Genre*. R. Howard, trans. Ithaca: Cornell Univ.

———. 1984. *Mikhail Bakhtin: The Dialogical Principle*. W. Godzich, trans. Minneapolis: Univ. of Minnesota.

Tompkins, Jane P. 1980. *Reader-response Criticism: From Formalism to Post-Structuralism*. Baltimore: Johns Hopkins.

Wiesel, Elie. 1976. *Messengers of God*. New York: Simon & Schuster.

Wills, Clair. 1989. "Upsetting the Public: Carnival, Hysteria, and Women's Texts." In *Bakhtin and Cultural Theory*. K. Hirschkopf and D. Shepherd, eds. Manchester: Manchester Univ.

INDEXES

AUTHORS

SUBJECTS